RSC
Swan Theatre

Sponsored by
Royal Insurance

Glen Loney (signature)

THE SILENT WOMAN or EPICOENE
by Ben Jonson

A programme/text with commentary by Simon Trussler

Contents

Swan Theatre Plays published by Methuen London
by arrangement with the Royal Shakespeare Company

D0166114

methuen

RSC

Royal Shakespeare Company

Sponsored by

Royal Insurance

The Royal Shakespeare Company (RSC), is the title under which the Royal Shakespeare Theatre, Stratford-upon-Avon, has operated since 1961. Now one of the best-known theatre companies in the world, the RSC builds on a long and distinguished history of theatre in Stratford-upon-Avon.

In essence, the aim of the Company is the same as that expressed in 1905 by Sir Frank Benson, then director of the Stratford theatre: 'to train a company, every member of which would be an essential part of a homogeneous whole, consecrated to the practice of the dramatic arts and especially to the representation of the plays of Shakespeare'. The RSC is formed around a core of associate artists — actors, directors, designers and others — with the aim that their different skills should combine, over the years, to produce a distinctive approach to theatre, both classical and modern.

The first permanent theatre in Stratford was built in 1875 but in 1926, just a year after the granting of its Royal Charter, this theatre was almost completely destroyed by fire. A worldwide campaign was launched to build a new one, and productions moved to a local cinema until the present theatre, designed by Elisabeth Scott, was opened by the Prince of Wales on 23 April, 1932. Over the next thirty years, under the influence of directors such as Robert Atkins, Bridges-Adams, Iden Payne, Komisarjevsky, Sir Barry Jackson, Glen Byam Shaw and Anthony Quayle, the Shakespeare Memorial Theatre maintained a worldwide reputation.

In 1960 under its newly-appointed artistic director, Peter Hall, the company extended its operations to include a London base at the Aldwych Theatre, and in 1961 it became the Royal Shakespeare Company. The repertoire widened to include modern as well as classical work, and other innovations of the period which have shaped today's Company were the travelling Theatre-go-round and experimental work which included the Theatre of Cruelty season.

Under Trevor Nunn, who took over as artistic director in 1968, this experimental work in small performance spaces led, in 1974, to the opening of The Other Place, Stratford-upon-Avon. This was a rehearsal space converted into a theatre and in 1977 its London counterpart, The Warehouse, opened with a policy of presenting new British plays. In the same year the RSC played its first season in Newcastle upon Tyne — now an annual event. In 1978, the year in which Terry Hands joined Trevor Nunn as Joint Artistic Director, the RSC also fulfilled an ambition to tour towns and villages with little or no access to live professional theatre.

In 1982, the RSC moved its London base to the Barbican Centre in the City of London, opening both the Barbican Theatre, specially built for the RSC by the generosity of the Corporation of the City of London, and The Pit, a small theatre converted like The Warehouse and The Other Place, from a rehearsal room.

The 1986 season saw the opening of the Swan. Built within the section of the shell of the original Shakespeare Memorial Theatre which escaped the 1926 fire, the Swan is a Jacobean-style playhouse staging mainly the work of dramatists from 1570-1750 — Shakespeare's contemporaries and successors whose work, once hugely popular, is now rarely performed. This new dimension to the Royal Shakespeare Company's work was made possible by the extremely generous gift of Frederick R. Koch, the RSC's benefactor.

In early 1987 Terry Hands became sole Artistic Director and Chief Executive of the Company.

In Spring 1989 the RSC's production of *Titus Andronicus,* which began life in the Swan, toured Europe, after performances at London's Riverside Studios.

Throughout its history, the RSC has augmented its central operations with national and international tours, films, television programmes, commercial transfers and fringe activities. Over the past 20 years, it has won over 200 national and international awards including most recently the Queen's Award for Export — but despite box office figures which, it is thought, have no equal anywhere in the world, the costs of RSC activities cannot be recouped from ticket sales alone. We rely on assistance from the Arts Council of Great Britain, amounting to about 30% of our costs in any one year, from work in other media and, increasingly, from commercial sponsorship. To find out more about the RSC's activities and to make sure of priority booking for our productions, why not become a member of the Company's Mailing List? Details of how to apply can be found in the theatre foyer or send SAE to Mailing List, Royal Shakespeare Theatre, Stratford-upon-Avon, CV37 6BB.

CAST IN ORDER OF APPEARANCE

Ned Clerimont, *a gentleman*	**Jared Harris**	Directed by	**Danny Boyle**
A Boy	**Liza Hayden**	Designed by	**Kandis Cook**
Truewit	**Richard McCabe**	Lighting by	**Rory Dempster**
Sir Dauphine Eugenie,	**Peter Hamilton Dyer**	Music by	**Barrington Pheloung**
a knight, nephew to Morose		Sound by	**Andrea J. Cox**
Sir Amorous La Foole,	**Michael Mears**	Company voice work by	**Cicely Berry** and
a knight			**Andrew Wade**
Morose,	**David Bradley**	Music Director	**Michael Tubbs**
a gentleman who hates noise		Assistant Director	**Matthew Richardson**
Mute, *Morose's servant*	**Graham Turner**	Stage Manager	**Michael Dembowicz**
Cutbeard, *a barber*	**William Chubb**	Deputy Stage Manager	**Ian Barber/**
Sir John Daw,	**John Ramm**		**Helen Lovat Fraser**
a knight, servant to Epicoene		Assistant Stage Manager	**Neil Constable**
Epicoene, *the silent woman*	**Hannah John**		
Master Otter,	**David Shaw-Parker**		
a land and sea captain			
Mistress Otter, *his wife*	**Jennie Heslewood**		
A Parson	**Paul Lacoux**		
Madame Haughty)*Ladies*	**Amanda Bellamy**		
Madame Centaur) *Collegiates*	**Rebecca Saire**		
Mistress (Dol) Mavis)	**Sarah Crowden**		
Mistress Trusty,	**Polly Kemp**		
Madame Haughty's woman			

Pages and servants played by
**Richard Doubleday, Michael Howell, Jacqueline
Leonard, William Oxborrow, Neil Richardson,
Georgia Slowe, Hilary Tones**

The performance is approximately 3 hours in length,
including one interval of 20 minutes.

First performance of this production: Swan Theatre, Stratford-upon-Avon, 28 June 1989.

**Please do not smoke or use cameras or tape recorders in the auditorium. And please remember that noise, such as whispering,
coughing, rustling programmes and the bleeping of digital watches can be distracting to performers and also spoils the
performance for other members of the audience.**

Arts Council Funded

Biographies

AMANDA BELLAMY *Madame Haughty*
Trained: RADA.
Theatre: Seasons at Sheffield, Salisbury, Manchester, Leatherhead, Cambridge, Harrogate, Bolton and Hull Truck Theatre Co. Elizabeth Bennet in *Pride and Prejudice*, Lady Macbeth in *Misalliance*, Hypatia Tarleton in *Misalliance*, Rosaline in *Love's Labour's Lost*, Olivia in *Twelfth Night*, Julia in *The Duchess of Malfi*, Toine in *Piaf*, Helena in *A Midsummer Night's Dream* (Repertory). Violette in *A Little Hotel on the Side* (NT). *Once a Catholic* (Sheffield Crucible tour), Jessica in *The Merchant of Venice* (British Council tour of Africa).
RSC: This season: Hermia in *A Midsummer Night's Dream*, Madame Haughty in *The Silent Woman or Epicoene*.
Television: *The Middle Ages* (BBC Schools Series), *Glorious Day*, *All in Good Faith*, *Terry and June*.
Film: *Little Dorrit*.

DANNY BOYLE *Director*
Theatre: Director of Theatre Upstairs, Royal Court (from 1981). Productions included *Up To The Sun*, *Panic*, *Salonika*, *Cinders*. Deputy Director of Royal Court 1983-86. Productions included *The Grace of Mary Traverse*, *Saved*, *The Genius*, *Victory* (also Joint Stock National Tour). *Two Planks And A Person* (Greenwich Theatre).
RSC: *The Bite of the Night*. This season: *The Silent Woman or Epicoene*, *H.I.D. (Hess is Dead)* (RSC/Almeida Season 1989).
Television: *Scout*, *The Venus de Milo* (winner of the 1987 San Francisco Television Festival), *The Rockingham Shoot*, *The Nightwatch*, *Monkeys: The Delorean Tapes*, *Elephant*, *The Hen House* (to be released).

DAVID BRADLEY *Morose*
Theatre: Includes Christ in York Mystery Plays (York). Milo in *Sleuth*, Edgar in *Lying Low* (King's Head), Desmond in *Funny Peculiar* (London). Bergetto in *'Tis Pity She's A Whore*, Schwarz in *The Front Page*, Trofimov in *The Cherry Orchard*, Sir Andrew Aguecheek in *Twelfth Night*, Claudio in *Measure for Measure* (NT).
RSC: Antonio in *The Merchant of Venice*, Matthew in *Captain Swing*, *The Swan Down Gloves*, Shakebag in *Arden of Faversham*, Albany in *King Lear*, Prison Doctor in Bond's *Lear*, Prologue/Charron in *Molière*, Openwork in *The Roaring Girl*, Cléante in *Tartuffe*, Dr. Jameson in *The Custom of the Country*, Camillo in *The Winter's Tale*, Dr. Caius in *The Merry Wives of Windsor*, *The Dillen*, Bartolomeo in *Il Candelaio*, Humpage in *A Penny for a Song*, Fistula in *Temptation*, Sir Andrew Aguecheek in *Twelfth Night*, title role in *Cymbeline*, Kulygin in *Three Sisters*. This season: Mephostophiles in *Dr. Faustus*, Morose in *The Silent Woman or Epicoene*.
Television: Includes *A Family at War*, *Another Sunday and Sweet FA*, *Bill Brand*, *Clapperclaw*, *One by One*, *The Pickersgill Primitive*, *Molière*, *Tartuffe*, *King of the Ghetto*, *Shadow of the Noose*, *Master of the Marionettes*.
Film: *Prick Up Your Ears*.

WILLIAM CHUBB *Cutbeard*
Theatre: Sherlock Holmes in *A Study in Scarlet* (Orchard Theatre), Demetrius in *A Midsummer Night's Dream*, Medley in *Man of Mode* (Cheek by Jowl, London & UK tour). *A Midsummer Night's Dream* (Cheek by Jowl tour to India, Europe & South America).
RSC: Solanio in *The Merchant of Venice*, Conrade in *Much Ado About Nothing* (RSC/Nat West Tour), Bat Burst in *The New Inn*, Decius/Titinius in *Julius Caesar*, Secretary in *Temptation*, Tailor in *The Taming of the Shrew*, Rode in *Three Sisters*, Jonathan John in *The Churchill Play*, Vanek in *Conversation* (May Fest '89). This season: Valdes/Pride/Cardinal of Lorraine/Duke of Vanholt in *Dr. Faustus*, Cutbeard in *The Silent Woman or Epicoene*.

SARAH CROWDEN *Mistress (Dol) Mavis*
Theatre: Seasons at Edinburgh Lyceum, Windsor, Worthing, Leeds and Derby.

Hon. Gwendolen Fairfax in *The Importance of Being Earnest*, Cecily in *84 Charing Cross Road*, Minnie in *the Matchmaker*, Edith the Maid in *Blithe Spirit*, *Now We Are Sixty*, Miss gossage in *The Happiest Days of Your Life* (Repertory). 1986 Cambridge Festival. *Cider With Rosie* (Greenwich), *Servant of Two Masters* (Croydon Warehouse). Mrs. Dunning in *Knuckle* (UK tour).
RSC: This season: Helena in *A Midsummer Night's Dream*, Mistress (Dol) Mavis in *The Silent Woman or Epicoene*.
Television: *David Copperfield*, *Swallows & Amazons for Ever*, *The Rainbow*, *Have His Carcase*, *Father Matthew's Daughter*, *The Oldest Goose in the Business*, *The Storyteller*, *Let's Pretend*, *Pig in the Middle*, *The Seven Dials Mystery*.
Film: *Erik the Viking*, *Billy the Kid and the Green Baize Vampire*, *Harem*, *Great Expectations*.

RORY DEMPSTER *Lighting Designer*
Theatre: Includes *Sizwe Bansi is Dead*, *The Island*, *Entertaining Mr. Sloane*, *City Sugar*, *Comedians*, *Teeth 'n Smiles*, *The Rocky Horror Show*, *All My Sons*, *Benefactors*, *The Interpreters* (West End). *The Cherry Orchard*, *The Changeling*, *Measure for Measure*, *A Moon for the Misbegotten* (Riverside). *Weapons of Happiness*, *The Madras House*, *Plenty*, *The Crucible*, *A Month in the Country*, *Serjeant Musgrave's Dance*, *Caritas*, *True West*, *Summer*, *A Map of the World*, *Road to Mecca*, *The Bay at Nice*, *King Lear* (National Theatre). *Dance of Death*, *Krapp's Last Tape* (Theater in Palast). *The Price*, *Diplomatic Wives* (Palace Theatre, Watford), Two productions for the Stichting Theatre Produktie in Rotterdam.
RSC: *Twelfth Night*, *Cousin Vladimir*, *The Bite of The Night*. This season: *The Silent Woman or Epicoene*.
Opera: Includes *Parsifal* (Royal Opera House).

RICHARD DOUBLEDAY *Page*
Trained: Guildford School of Acting.
Theatre: *The Magic Carpet*, *Frankenstein* (Polka Children's Theatre, Wimbledon).
RSC: Plebeian in *Julius Caesar*, Youth/Gendarme in *Bite of the Night*, Prisoner/Police Officer in *Measure for Measure*, George Lamacraft in *The Churchill Play*. This season: Paris' Page in *Romeo and Juliet*, Lechery/Paramour in *Dr. Faustus*, *The Silent Woman or Epicoene*.

PETER HAMILTON DYER *Sir Dauphine Eugenie*
Trained: Central School of Speech and Drama.
Theatre: Seasons at Harrogate including Craig in *The Normal Heart*, Nigel in *Adrian Mole*, Angelo and Theo in *Piaf*. Pentheus in *The Bacchae* (Lyric Hammersmith and UK tour with Shared Experience).
RSC: This season: Lord/Fairy in *A Midsummer Night's Dream*, Sir Dauphine Eugenie in *The Silent Woman or Epicoene*.
Television: *Dr. Who*
Other: Narrator for The London Chorale. Member of The Actors and Writers Workshop.

JOHN HANNAH *Epicoene*
Theatre: Gus in *Waiting for Shuggie's Ma* (Royal Court), Johnnie in *The Gorbals Story* (Glasgow Citizens) John in *The Philanthropist* (Mobil Tour), Caspian in *Voyage of the Dawn Treader*, Bandy Corner in *The Gambling Man*, Robert in *Rents* (Newcastle Playhouse), Phil in *Rents* (Palace Theatre Westcliffe), Pie McKay/Susie Creamcheese in *The Innocent* (Traverse Theatre), Jerry in *The Zoo Story* (Tron Theatre), Malcolm in *Macbeth* (Royal Exchange), Joe in *The Daughter-in-Law* (Bristol Old Vic).
RSC: This season: Epicoene in *The Silent Woman or Epicoene*.
Television: *Pretty Boy* in *Reasonable Force*, Johnny in *Bookie*, *Brief Encounter*, Robert in *Brond*, Keith in *These Colours Don't Run*.
Film: Tommy in *Losers Blues*.

JARED HARRIS *Clerimont*
Trained: Central School of Speech and Drama.

Theatre: *Treasure Island* (Clwyd Repertory).
RSC: This season: Gregory/Third Watch in *Romeo and Juliet*, Fortinbras in *Hamlet*, Clerimont in *The Silent Woman or Epicoene*.
Film: Geoff in *The Rachel Papers* (U.A./Virgin)

LIZA HAYDEN *The Boy*
Trained: Corona Academy.
Theatre: Seasons at Newcastle Playhouse. Lucy in *The Lion the .Witch and the Wardrobe*, Annabelle in *The Pirate Queen*, Charo in *Hotel Dorado* (Repertory).
RSC: Gavroche in *Les Misérables*. This season: Fairy in *A Midsummer Night's Dream*, The Boy in *The Silent Woman or Epicoene*.
Television: *I Claudius, Bavarian Nights, The Shadow Cage, Letter Writing, King and Castle, Blind Justice, Casualty, Shine on Harvey Moon, Dempsey and Makepeace.*
Radio: *Brat Farrah, Patterson, Leave Me Alone, The Buckingham Palace Connections.*

JENNIE HESLEWOOD *Mistress Otter*
Trained: Central School of Speech and Drama.
Theatre: Seasons at Flora Robson Playhouse, Ipswich and the National Theatre. *Armstrong's Last Goodnight, Miss Julie, Much Ado About Nothing, Trelawny of the Wells, Royal Hunt of the Sun* (NT). *Women Beware Women* (Arts Theatre), *Fire Raisers* (Royal Court). Prospect Productions, *The Confederacy* (UK Tours, National Theatre).
RSC: This season: Lady in *Romeo and Juliet*, Mistress Otter in *The Silent Woman or Epicoene*.
Television: *Penda's Fen, Omnibus — Vanity Fair.*

MICHAEL HOWELL *Servant*
Born: Oxford.
Theatre: First work in the theatre.
RSC: This season: Paris in *Romeo and Juliet*, Sailor in *Hamlet*, Servant in *The Silent Woman or Epicoene*.

POLLY KEMP *Mistress Trusty*
Trained: The Drama Centre, London.
RSC: This season: Fairy in *Midsummer Night's Dream*, Mistress Trusty in *The Silent Woman or Epicoene*.

PAUL LACOUX *Parson*
Trained: Bristol Old Vic Theatre School.
Theatre: Seasons at Pitlochry Festival Theatre and The Wolsey Theatre, Bristol. Jack Absolute in *The Rivals*, James Harthouse in *Hard Times*, Greg in *Relatively Speaking*, Bunny in *Mr. Cinders*. Paco in *Short Eyes* (The Man in the Moon), Cantavalle in *Naked* (Old Red Lion).
RSC: This season: Demetrius in *A Midsummer Night's Dream*, Osric in *Hamlet*, Parson in *The Silent Woman or Epicoene*.
Television: *Casualty, The Singing Detective, Fortunes of War, Sherlock Holmes, The Casebook of Hercule Poirot.*
Film: *Casanova.*

JACQUELINE LEONARD *Servant*
Trained: L.A.M.D.A.
Theatre: Seasons at Mercury Theatre, Colchester including Bianca in *The Taming of the Shrew*, Helena in *Look Back in Anger*.
RSC: This season: Fairy in *A Midsummer Night's Dream*, Servant in *The Silent Woman or Epicoene*.

RICHARD McCABE *Truewit*
Theatre: Seasons at Sheffield Crucible, Bolton, Manchester Royal Exchange. *Renaissance, The Alchemist, The Changeling* (Sheffield Crucible), *Should Auld Acquaintance*, Mozart in *Amadeus* (Bolton Octagon), Simon in *Hay Fever*, Touchstone in *As You Like It* (Royal Exchange, Manchester & UK tour), *Pistols*

(Theatre Royal, Plymouth), Mercutio in *Romeo and Juliet* (Leeds Playhouse), *Some of My Best Friends Are Husbands* (Leicester Haymarket & UK tour).
RSC: Bentley Summerhays in *Misalliance*, Sir Glorious Tipto in *The New Inn*, Lacy in *Hyde Park*, Chiron in *Titus Andronicus*, Jimmy Umpleby in *The Churchill Play*. This season: Puck in *A Midsummer Night's Dream*, Truewit in *The Silent Woman or Epicoene*, Wagner in *Dr. Faustus*.
Television: *The Bill, Bulman.*

MICHAEL MEARS *Sir Amorous la Foole*
Trained: Drama Centre
Theatre: Bassanio in *The Merchant of Venice*, Fagin in *Oliver*, Young Marlow in *She Stoops to Conquer*, Don Quixote in *The Trarails of Sancho Panza*, both the Kray Twins in *Glitterballs*, Felix in *The Normal Heart*. Season at Leeds Playhouse: Kafka in *Kafka's Dick*, the lead in *Intimate Exchanges*. West End credits include *i* (Picadilly Theatre), Malvolio in *Twelfth Night (ATC)*.
RSC: This season: Sir Amorous la Foole in *The Silent Woman or Epicoene*.
Television: *Reilly, Raspberry Ripple, Shout Aloud Salvation, Chelmsford 123, The Lenny Henry Show.*
Film: *Down the Valley, Car Trouble, Little Dorrit, Queen of Hearts, A Man Called Sarge.*

WILLIAM OXBORROW *Servant*
Trained: LAMDA.
RSC: Francisco in *Hamlet* (RSC/RI Tour 1988). This season: Francisco in *Hamlet*, Balthasar in *Romeo and Juliet*, Servant in *The Silent Woman or Epicoene*.

DAVID SHAW-PARKER *Master Otter*
Born: Abyad, Egypt. **Trained:** RADA.
Theatre: Bardolph in *Henry V*, Casca in *Julius Caesar*, De Stogumber in *Saint Joan*, Waitwell in *Way of the World*, Thomas Beckett in *Murder in the Cathedral*, Dr. Herder in *The Ruling Class*, Demon King in *Jack and the Beanstalk*, Merriman in *The Importance of Being Earnest*, O'Hara in *Arsenic and Old Lace*, Bertram in *A Little Night Music*, Mr. Purdue in *Habeas Corpus*, Unc Nunkie in *Patchwork Girl of Oz*, Musician in *Caucasian Chalk Circle*, Moses in *School for Scandal*, Mo in *Born in the Gardens* (Repertory). Marinito in *Trial by Fire*, Tommy in *Milkwood Blues*, Solo appearance in *Bond Songs* (Lyric Hammersmith). Arthur in *Up 'n Under*, God in *A Fine Romance* (London West End). Narrator in *A Family Album* (Vienna).
RSC: Jamy in *Henry V*, Sir John Sommerville/Clerk of Chatham/Son who killed his father in *Henry VI Parts 1, 2 & 3*, William in *As You Like It*, Volscian in *Coriolanus* (European tour), Servant in *The Changeling*, The Artist in *Saratoga*, Barry Singer in *A & R*, Interrogator in *Savage Amusement*, Francis/Silence in *Henry IV*, George Seacoal in *Much Ado About Nothing*, Ballon in *Peer Gynt*, De Lessac in *Molière*, Biondello in *The Taming of the Shrew*, Gilbert in *The Body*, Pons/The Elder in *Soft Cops*, Bellerose in *Cyrano de Bergerac* (London, New York, L.A. & Broadway). This season: Snout in *A Midsummer Night's Dream*, Master Otter in *The Silent Woman or Epicoene*, Evil Angel/Envy/The Pope/Horse-courser in *Dr. Faustus*.
Television: *I Woke Up One Morning, Inspector Morse, The Bill, Crossroads, P.C. Pinkerton, Cyrano de Bergerac, Molière, Bondsongs, Arena — Hands Off the Classics, The Brolly's.*
Radio: *King Lear, Molière, Plutus, Romeo and Juliet, The Confidential Clerk, A Winter Story, Trial By Fire.*
Composing/Recordings: *The War Plays* (RSC), *Derek* (RSC and Thames TV). Recorded *Bondsongs* (J.J. Records).

BARRINGTON PHELOUNG *Composer*
Theatre: Includes *Two Planks and a Person* (Greenwich), *Made in Bangkok* (Aldwych), *The Foreigner* (Albery), *Sweet Bird of Youth* (USA).
RSC: *Bite of the Night*. This season: *The Silent Woman or Epicoene*.
Television: *Run Like Thunder, What if it's Raining?, Exit no Exit, Lovebirds, My Kingdom for a Horse, Saracen, Boon.*
Radio: *Helix, Two Planks and a Person* (new score).
Films: *Inspector Morse, Friendship's Death*, Videos for the Design Council.

JOHN RAMM *Sir John Daw*

Trained: Webber Douglas Academy.
Theatre: Bernie in *Sexual Perversity in Chicago*, Raoul in *The Phantom of the Opera*, Dionysus in *The Bacchae* (ETC). Edgar Beagly in *The House of Usher* (Theatre West), Fool in *The Fool* (Edinburgh Fringe Festival), The Pardoner in *The Canterbury Tales*, Constable in *Accidental Death of an Anarchist*, Venticelli in *Amadeus*, Happy in *Death of a Salesman*, Jack in *Cider with Rosie*, Partridge in *The History of Tom Jones*, Feste in *Twelfth Night*, Peter in *Zoo Story*, Autolycus in *The Winter's Tale*, Fireman in *The Bald Prima Donna*, Husband in *The Breasts of Tiresias*, Oberon in *The Park*, Yasha in *The Cherry Orchard* (Crucible Theatre Sheffield).
RSC: Laertes in *Hamlet* (RSC/RI tour 1988). This season: Laertes in *Hamlet*, Sir John Daw in *The Silent Woman or Epicoene*.
Television: *The Wall Game*, *Let's Pretend*, *South of the Border*.

MATTHEW RICHARDSON *Assistant Director*

Theatre: Lighting Designer at the Royal Court, Riverside Studios, Old Vic and Almeida Theatre where he also spent a year as Technical Director. Assistant Director on *The Possessed* (Almeida Theatre and Theatre of Europe).
RSC: *Hamlet* (RSC/RI tour 1988). This season: *A Midsummer Night's Dream*, *Hamlet*, *The Silent Woman or Epicoene*.
Opera: Lighting Designer for several companies including English National Opera, Welsh National Opera, Scottish Opera, Opera North, Staff Director for Scottish Opera 1985/86 season. Assistant Director on *Madam Butterfly* (Scottish Opera/ Royal Opera House). Directed *Apollo and Daphne* (Batignano Opera Festival Italy), *Tales of Hoffmann*, *The Marriage of Figaro* (Scottish Opera), *Jenûfa* (Scottish Opera-go-Round). *Eis Thanaton* (City of Birmingham Touring Opera at Cheltenham Festival), *Carmen* (Opera 80).

NEIL RICHARDSON *Servant*

Trained: Central School of Speech and Drama.
Theatre: *She Stoops to Conquer* (Southwold Repertory Co and Jill Freud UK tour)
RSC: This season: Fairy/Lord in *A Midsummer Night's Dream*, Marcellus in *Hamlet*, Servant in *The Silent Woman or Epicoene*.

REBECCA SAIRE *Madame Centaur*

Theatre: Seasons at The Mill Theatre, Sonning and Redgrave Theatre, Farnham. Polly Meara in *The Gingerbread Lady*, Laura in *The Glass Menagerie* (Repertory). Work in London includes Louise in *Thunder in the Air* (Gate), May in *The Ticket-of-leave-Man* (NT), Beatrice in *I and Albert* (Piccadilly).
RSC: Madeline Bray in *Nicholas Nickleby* (also USA tour). This season: Ophelia in *Hamlet*, Madame Centaur in *The Silent Woman or Epicoene*.
Television: *Romeo and Juliet*, *Love in a Cold Climate*, *The Schoolmistress*, *Family Theatre* (USA), *A.D.*, *Starting Out*, *Vanity Fair*, *A Taste for Death*.
Radio: *Rumpole*, *The Senses*.
Film: *The Shooting Party*.

GEORGIA SLOWE *Servant*

Theatre: Pamela in *Five Finger Exercise* (Cambridge Theatre Co), Juliet in *Romeo and Juliet* (Temba Theatre Co).
RSC: This season: Juliet in *Romeo and Juliet*, Servant in *The Silent Woman or Epicoene*.
Television: *The Mill on the Floss*, *The Enchanted Castle*, *Mackenzie*, *Marco Polo*, *The Confessions of Felix Krull*, *Fraulein Else*, *You'll Never See Me Again*, *A.D.*, *Wallenberg — The Lost Hero*, *I'll take Manhattan*, *Boon — Paper Mafia*, *The Attic — The Hiding of Anne Frank*.
Film: *Secret Places*, *The Company of Wolves*, *The Inquiry*.

HILARY TONES *Servant*

Trained: Central School of Speech and Drama.
Theatre: Sybil Merton in *Lord Arthur Saville's Crime* (Empty Space Theatre Co at Man in the Moon & Latchmere). UK tours with Bedside Manners Touring Co. Tours abroad include Celia in *As You Like It* (Stratford Connecticut USA), Cecily in *The Importance of Being Earnest*, Grumio in *The Taming of the Shrew* (Holland, Germany & Belgium), Lady Macduff in *Macbeth* (Norway).
RSC: This season: Rosaline in *Romeo and Juliet*, Lady in *Hamlet*, Servant in *The Silent Woman or Epicoene*.
Television: *Gaudy Night*.

MICHAEL TUBBS *Music Director*

Education: Cambridge University, Guildhall School of Music.
Theatre: After five years working in repertory theatres, joined RSC as Deputy Music Director in 1967. Music Director for most productions at the RST and several at The Other Place and Swan Theatre since then. Arranged the music for *Twelfth Night*, *Piaf*, *The Suicide*. Wrote music for The Other Place's first production — Buzz Goodbody's *King Lear*.

GRAHAM TURNER *Mute*

Theatre: Tim in *Noises Off* (Leicester Haymarket), Louis in *Leave Him to Heaven* (Nuffield Theatre Southampton), The Brother in *As Is* (Half Moon), The Public (Stratford East). Paul in *A Chorus Line* (Theatre Royal Drury Lane).
RSC: Rowland in *The Witch of Edmonton*, Tommy Taylor in *The Dillen*, Cyril in *Mary After the Queen*, Peter Simple in *The Merry Wives of Windsor*, Barra in *Il Candelaio*. Title role in *Johnny Johnson*, *Stitch* (Not the RSC Festival, Almeida Theatre). Dion in *The Winter's Tale*, Herrick in *The Crucible* (RSC/RI Tour 1984). *All's Well That Ends Well* (New York). This season: Flute in *A Midsummer Night's Dream*, Mute in *The Silent Woman or Epicoene*, Clown/Sloth/Ralph in *Dr. Faustus*.
Television: *The Devil's Disciple*, *Casualty*, *Sweet As You Are*, *Grange Hill*.

UNDERSTUDIES
William Chubb *Morose*
Sarah Crowden *Mistress Otter*
Richard Doubleday *John Daw/Cutbeard*
Michael Howell *Clerimont/la Foole*
Polly Kemp *Mavis*
Paul Lacoux *Dauphine*
Jacqueline Leonard *Madame Centaur*
Michael Mears *Truewit*
William Oxborrow *Epicoene*
Neil Richardson *Otter/Parson*
Georgia Slowe *Mistress Trusty/Boy*
Hilary Tones *Madame Haughty*

Royal Shakespeare Company

Sponsored by
Royal Insurance

STRATFORD-UPON-AVON Box Office 0789 295623

30 March–2 September 1989

ROYAL SHAKESPEARE THEATRE

A MIDSUMMER NIGHT'S DREAM
by William Shakespeare
Directed by John Caird

HAMLET
by William Shakespeare
Directed by Ron Daniels

CYMBELINE
by William Shakespeare
Directed by Bill Alexander

SWAN THEATRE

ROMEO AND JULIET
by William Shakespeare
Directed by Terry Hands

DR FAUSTUS
by Christopher Marlowe
Directed by Barry Kyle

THE SILENT WOMAN or EPICOENE
by Ben Jonson
Directed by Danny Boyle

THE OTHER PLACE

7 August for 6 weeks
OTHELLO
by William Shakespeare
Directed by Trevor Nunn

Transferring to The Young Vic

18 September for 8 weeks
Box Office 01-928 6363

Public booking opens 17 July

LONDON Box Office 01-638 8891

18 March–4 November 1989

BARBICAN THEATRE

THE PLANTAGENETS
adapted from William Shakespeare's
Henry VI Parts I, II and III and Richard III as
**HENRY VI, The Rise of EDWARD IV,
RICHARD III, his Death**
Directed by Adrian Noble

Until 31 August
MACBETH
by William Shakespeare
Directed by Adrian Noble

THE TEMPEST
by William Shakespeare
Directed by Nicholas Hytner

12 July–12 September
THE MAN WHO CAME TO DINNER
by Moss Hart and George S. Kaufman
Directed by Gene Saks

From 21 September
THE MASTER BUILDER
by Henrik Ibsen
Directed by Adrian Noble

THE PIT

KING JOHN
by William Shakespeare
Directed by Deborah Warner

Supported by

Until 5 August
THE MAN OF MODE
by George Etherege
Directed by Garry Hynes

12 July–12 September
SOME AMERICANS ABROAD
by Richard Nelson
Directed by Roger Michell

From 26 July
ACROSS OKA
by Robert Holman
Directed by Sarah Pia Anderson

From 16 August
THE LOVE OF THE NIGHTINGALE
by Timberlake Wertenbaker
Directed by Garry Hynes

From 20 September
MARY AND LIZZIE
by Frank McGuinness
Directed by Sarah Pia Anderson

ALMEIDA THEATRE
Box Office 01-359 4404
13 September–28 October

From 13 September
KING LEAR
by William Shakespeare
Directed by Cicely Berry

From 19 September
KISSING THE POPE
by Nick Darke
Directed by Roger Michell

From 20 September
H.I.D. (Hess is Dead)
by Howard Brenton
Directed by Danny Boyle

RSC IN THE WEST END

PALACE THEATRE Box Office 01-437 8834
LES MISERABLES
by Alain Boublil, Claude-Michel
Schönberg and Herbert Kretzmer

AMBASSADORS THEATRE
Box Office 01-836 6111
LES LIAISONS DANGEREUSES
by Christopher Hampton

RSC

Swan Theatre

Sponsored by
Royal Insurance

Royal Shakespeare Company
Incorporated under Royal Charter as the
Royal Shakespeare Theatre
Patron Her Majesty the Queen
President Sir Kenneth Cork
Chairman of the Council Geoffrey A Cass
Vice Chairman Dennis L Flower
Advisory Direction Peggy Ashcroft, Peter Brook, Trevor Nunn
Artistic Director and Chief Executive Terry Hands
Direction Bill Alexander, John Barton, John Caird, Ron Daniels,
Terry Hands, Barry Kyle, Adrian Noble
Director Emeritus Trevor Nunn
Artistic Director 1989 London Season Adrian Noble
Company Director 1989 Stratford Spring Season Ron Daniels

Administration
John Bradley *Technical Services Administrator*
David Brierley *General Manager*
Stephen Browning *Head of Marketing, Press and Publicity*
James Langley *Production Controller*
Carol Malcolmson *Planning Administrator*
Genista McIntosh *Senior Administrator*
James Sargant *Barbican Administrator*
William Wilkinson *Financial Controller*

Heads of Department
Cicely Berry *Voice*
Siobhan Bracke *Casting*
Colin Chambers *Literary*
Brian Davenhill *Scenic Workshops*
Susan Davenport *Sponsorship*
David Fletcher *Accounts*
Andy Henson *Data Processing*
Tony Hill *Education*
Brenda Leedham *Wigs and Make-up*
William Lockwood *Property Shop*
Nigel Loomes *Paint Shop*
Peter Pullinger *Construction*
Frances Roe *Wardrobe*
John Watts *Management Services Coordinator*
Guy Woolfenden *Music*

RSC Collection
Brian Glover *Director*

Swan Theatre
Peter Cholerton *Property Master*
Mark Collins *Master Carpenter*
Sonia Dosanjh *Company Manager*
Wayne Dowdeswell *Chief Electrician*
Josie Horton *Deputy Wardrobe Mistress*
Geoff Locker *Production Manager*
Stuart McCann *Property Dayman*
Chris Millard *Press (0789) 296655*
Chris Neale *House Manager*
Richard Power *Deputy Chief Electrician*
Eileen Relph *House Manager*
Richard Rhodes *Deputy Theatre Manager*
Graham Sawyer *Theatre Manager and Licensee*
Ursula Selbiger *Box Office Manager*
Sian Stirling *Publicity*
David Sutton *Stage Dayman*
Michael Tubbs *Director of Music*
John Woolf *Music Director*

Facilities
In addition to bar and coffee facilities on the ground floor, there is wine
on sale on the first floor bridge outside Gallery 1. Toilets, including
facilities for disabled people, are situated on the ground floor only.

RSC Collection
Over a thousand items on view: costumes, props, pictures and sound
recordings illustrating the changes in staging from medieval times to the
use of the thrust stage in the Swan, and comparisons of past productions
of the current season's plays. Come and see our exhibition; browse in
the sales and refreshments area — and book a theatre tour.
Open 9.15am - 8pm, Sundays 12 noon - 5pm.

Production Acknowledgements
Scenery, properties, costumes and wigs made in RST Workshops,
Stratford-upon-Avon. Backcloth painted by Alastair Brotchie. Swan
Property Manager Mark Graham.

The Silent Woman:
a Critical Commentary
by Simon Trussler

The Compiler

Simon Trussler has contributed the commentaries to thirteen previous volumes in Methuen's Swan Theatre Plays series. He has been an editor of *New Theatre Quarterly* and its predecessor *Theatre Quarterly* since 1971, and presently teaches in the Drama Department of Goldsmiths' College, University of London. *Shakespearean Concepts*, just published by Methuen, is the latest of nearly two dozen books on theatrical subjects he has written or edited. He is also General Editor of the Methuen 'Writer-File' series, and was founding-editor of the Royal Shakespeare Company's *Yearbook* in 1978, compiling the annual editions until 1985.

Stage History

The first performance of *Epicoene, or The Silent Woman*, was, according to its original title-page, 'acted in the year 1609 by the Children of His Majesty's Revels' — presumably in December, or early in the following month (still 1609, according to the 'old style' calendar), at the Whitefriars playhouse, where the boy company had just taken up residence. By February, the play had been suppressed, following the complaint from the king's cousin discussed on page xvi, and we have no details of further performances in the regular theatres for half a century. But records of two revivals at court during the 1630s suggest that the play had been restored to the repertoire, and it was among the first to be staged after the Restoration in 1660, with Edward Kynaston taking the title-role — though it soon became traditional for an actress to play the part. For almost a century the piece remained highly popular, but it evidently proved less of an attraction in Garrick's revival of 1752, and in 1776 he commissioned George Colman to provide an expurgated version — also restoring an actor to the role of Epicoene, though Sarah Siddons took it for a few performances. Since the Covent Garden production of 1784, the only professional revival in London has been that by the Phoenix Society at the Regent in 1924, when, according to James Agate, Godfrey Winn 'looked well' as Epicoene.

Synopsis

Truewit, discovering his friend Clerimont at his toilet, laments the misfortunes of their fellow-gallant Dauphine, whose uncle Morose is obsessively fearful of noise — and now, as Dauphine arrives to tell them, is planning to marry a 'silent woman' found for him by his barber Cutbeard, and so disinherit Dauphine by begetting an heir. The foppish Sir Amorous La Foole appears with an invitation for them all to dine at Captain Otter's, where they will be able to meet not only the 'silent woman', Mistress Epicoene, but the members of the so-called 'college' of ladies, 'an order between courtiers and country madams', whose Amazonian behaviour belies their readiness to bend before every fashionable opinion.

At his lodgings, Morose is instructing his servant in the arts of silence when Truewit bursts in to proclaim as noisily as he can the disadvantages of marriage. Dauphine is meanwhile enjoying the spectacle of the would-be scholar Sir John Daw garrulously proclaiming the virtues of silence to Epicoene: but his amusement turns to consternation when Truewit enters to boast of his stratagem — for, as Dauphine now informs his friends, Epicoene has assured him of a slice of his uncle's fortune once they are married. However, Cutbeard arrives with news that Morose believes Dauphine to have been behind Truewit's dissuasions, and is now more intent than ever upon matrimony.

Introduced to Epicoene in person, Morose is charmed by her modesty — but once the marriage ceremony is over, he finds that his bride has, after all, a sharp tongue and a far from submissive nature. His consternation is compounded by the arrival of all the gallants, gulls, and ladies, determined upon a riotous celebration of the nuptials. While the collegiate ladies take Epicoene to their bosoms, the young men plot to deceive Daw and La Foole — first to rivalry, and then to panic at the prospect of having to fight a duel, which they avoid only to their mutual dishonour and discomfort.

Meanwhile, Cutbeard and Otter have disguised themselves as lawyers, and discourse loudly and at length to Morose on every possible ground for the divorce he now heartily desires. But despite Morose's false confession of his impotence, and a no less false confession from Daw and La Foole that they have both lain with Epicoene, no solution can be found — until Dauphine offers to release his uncle from his torment in return for an annual income and the assurance of becoming his heir. Morose readily agrees to this — and some surprising revelations follow.

Ben Jonson: a Brief Chronology

1572 Born, 11 June, a month after the death of his father. His mother remarried a master-bricklayer of Westminster, *c*. 1575, and Jonson was 'brought up poorly' in his early childhood.

1583 *c*. Educated at Westminster School under his lifelong friend, the scholar William Camden, until *c*. 1588.

1591 *c*. After a brief and unhappy apprenticeship to his stepfather, went as a volunteer to fight for the Dutch against the Spanish in Flanders.

1594 Married Anne Lewis, 'a shrew yet honest'.

1596 Birth of his first son, Benjamin.

1597 Became an actor and jobbing playwright in London under the manager Philip Henslowe. August-October, imprisoned for his share in the 'lewd', 'seditious' lost comedy *The Isle of Dogs*.

1598 *The Case Is Altered* performed by the Children of the Chapel. First success with *Every Man in His Humour* for the Lord Chamberlain's Men. Killed Gabriel Spencer, a fellow actor, in a duel, for which he was imprisoned (pleading 'benefit of clergy') and his goods confiscated. Became a Catholic in prison.

1599 Collaborated with Dekker and others on the lost tragedies *Page of Plymouth* and *Robert II, King of Scots*. *Every Man out of His Humour* played by Lord Chamberlain's Men. Birth of his second son, Joseph.

1600 The 'war of the theatres', to which Jonson contributed *Cynthia's Revels* and *Poetaster*, both for the Chapel Children.

1601 Revisions to Kyd's *The Spanish Tragedy* for Henslowe.

1602 Living successively with Sir Robert Townshend and in the household of Lord D'Aubigny, during separation of five years from his wife.

1603 Accession of James I. Jonson wrote his first royal entertainment, the *King's Entertainment at Althorp*, but was also called before the Privy Council to answer for suspected papist tendencies in *Sejanus*, his unsuccessful tragedy for the King's Men (as Chamberlain's now known). Death of his son Benjamin.

1605 His first masque, *The Masque of Blackness*, performed at court, but his collaboration with Marston and Chapman on *Eastward Ho!* (played by Queen's Revels at Blackfriars) landed him again in prison. Minor involvement in Gunpowder Plot.

1606 The masque *Hymenaei* performed at court, and *Volpone* by King's Men at the Globe. Summoned for recusancy.

1608 Continuing to write court masques and other entertainments. Second son to be named Benjamin born.

1609 *Epicoene* played by the Children of Whitefriars.

1610 *The Alchemist* played by the King's Men. About this time Jonson returned to the Anglican faith.

1611 Second and last tragedy, *Catiline* (performed by King's Men), also a failure. He was continuing throughout this period to write masques and entertainments, this year's being *The Masque of Oberon* and *Love Freed from Ignorance and Folly*.

1612 Travelled to France as tutor to son of Sir Walter Raleigh.

1614 Lady Elizabeth's stage *Bartholomew Fair* at the Hope.

1616 Granted annual pension of one hundred marks by the king. Performance of *The Devil Is an Ass* by King's Men at the Blackfriars, after which Jonson devoted his energies for next nine years to writing for the court. Published his *Works* in folio.

1618 Walked from London to Scotland to visit the poet Drummond of Hawthornden, who recorded their *Conversations*.

1619 Made honorary Master of Arts by Oxford University.

1623 Fire in Jonson's lodgings destroyed his books and manuscripts. Contributed a verse tribute to the First Folio of Shakespeare's collected works.

1624 Projected court performance of his masque *Neptune's Triumph* cancelled, partly because of its reflections upon Prince Charles's failed plans for a Spanish marriage.

1626 First of Jonson's final group of comedies, *The Staple of News*, for the King's Men at the Blackfriars.

1628 Confined to his chambers by a paralytic stroke.

1629 Failure of *The New Inn* at the Blackfriars.

1631 Brief return to masque writing with *Love's Triumph through Callipolis* and *Chloridia*, but his squabbles with Inigo Jones over style and precedence again lost him favour at court.

1632 *The Magnetic Lady*, probably his last comedy, played by the King's Men.

1633 *A Tale of a Tub*, conjecturally a revised version of an early and previously unperformed play, staged by Queen Henrietta's Men at the Cockpit.

1634 Final royal entertainment, *Love's Welcome at Bolsover*. Jonson was increasingly destitute in these last years.

1637 Died on 6 August, and buried in Westminster Abbey.

The Theatres of Ben Jonson

Unlike Shakespeare, who spent most of his working life as an actor, shareholder, and, of course, 'ordinary poet' for a single company, Ben Jonson was a free-lance — a theatrical mercenary who sold his services wherever he could command his fee. And by the early years of the seventeenth century, his work had already been seen in every one of the available 'public' theatres in London — those open-air houses, where the groundlings stood around a raised thrust stage on three sides, while the enclosing tiers of galleries provided seating (and some protection from the elements) for patrons with an extra penny or two to spare.

Thus, Jonson's earliest hackwork in the 1590s was for Philip Henslowe, the canny impresario who at that time was running the Rose Theatre on Bankside, where the Lord Admiral's Men was the resident company. Close by was the Swan, where in 1597 Jonson had a hand in the revision of *The Isle of Dogs* which brought down the wrath of the authorities both on the performing company, Pembroke's Men, and on Jonson himself. His earliest acknowledged play, *Every Man in His Humour*, was written in 1598 for the long-standing rivals to the Admiral's, the Lord Chamberlain's Men, who were then probably playing at the Curtain, in London's northern 'theatre district' of Shoreditch, following their occupancy of the original Theatre nearby. But in 1599 they moved south of the river to the newly-built Globe, where *Every Man out of His Humour* was one of the first plays to be performed. In the following year, Henslowe crossed the Thames in the opposite direction, to Finsbury, where he opened the new Fortune Theatre — in which Jonson's revisions to Kyd's *The Spanish Tragedy* would first have reached the stage.

In due course, a play by Jonson, *Bartholomew Fair*, was also to be among the first produced at the next and last of the public playhouses to be built in London — the Hope, opened in 1614 on the site of the old Bear Garden so beloved of Captain Otter in *The Silent Woman*. In between, two other of the comic master-pieces of Jonson's vintage period, *Volpone* and *The Alchemist*, were played at the Globe by the King's Men — as the Lord Chamberlain's were known after receiving James's personal patronage in 1603. But *The Silent Woman*, like the satires which formed Jonson's contributions to the 'war of the theatres', were played by children's companies — those unfledged 'little eyases' whose popularity had caused the players in *Hamlet* to try their fortunes abroad.

The circumstances of the children's companies, and the nature of the plays they performed, were central to the conception and, indeed, the reception of our play: and I discuss these separately, on page xiii, below. Here, it need only be stressed that all performed in theatres quite different from those of the adult players. These were indoor playhouses, which required artificial lighting, and where seats were provided in the so-called pit area — which became the most fashionable part of the house. Considerably smaller in capacity, the indoor theatres are often said to have attracted a 'coterie' audience. If it was indeed such, shared taste and, of course, ability to pay the higher prices for admission were the limiting factors, not any formal exclusiveness such as the description of these theatres as 'private' perhaps suggests. Indeed, the origins of this term are now uncertain. Possibly it derived from the end-on staging in the indoor theatres, which more nearly resembled playing conditions in the houses of wealthy citizens where itinerant players had earlier performed: other explanations include the need of the managers of the boy companies to conceal the economic exploitation of their charges as best they could, or simply a hope that the description would enable them to evade the licensing restrictions allowed to 'private houses' in the domestic sense.

Be this as it may, it is certain, at least, that these theatres were somehow able to evade the prohibition upon playing within the City of London, which had driven the adult companies into the northern and southern suburbs. It had presumably been in the hopes of surmounting these restrictions that James Burbage had taken a lease on a suitable space within the former monastery of Blackfriars and converted it into a theatre in 1596 — only to be forced into assigning it to the Children of the Chapel when he was unable to obtain the necessary permission. Paradoxically, it was in 1608, when the so-called 'liberty' of Blackfriars was transferred from royal jurisdiction to the control of the City, that the prohibition was at last overcome. The children's company consequently had to move further west, to the premises in the Whitefriars where *The Silent Woman* was first performed, and the King's Men began to use the Blackfriars for their winter seasons at some time after the ending of the plague restrictions of 1609. Thereafter, new playhouses intended for the adult companies were mostly built on similar lines, and both the Phoenix Theatre, converted from a cockpit in Drury Lane in 1616, and the Salisbury Court, opened in 1629, were 'private' or indoor houses, establishing the pattern of theatre building as it continued to evolve after the Restoration.

Both boy and adult players also took their work to what was, in effect, London's 'third theatre', the court of King James: and here, too, Jonson enjoyed success — not least in 1609, the year of *The Silent Woman*, and of the plague which, for much of the time, closed 'public' and 'private' theatres alike.

The Playwright and the Plague Year

When, almost too frequently, biographers quote Beaumont's lines, addressed to Jonson, in which he recalls 'What things we have seen / Done at the Mermaid', it is usually as anecdotal evidence for our dramatist's supposed love of canary wine and good company. But no less significant was the occasion of this 'occasional poem'. For Beaumont was writing nostalgically from the country — where he had fled in part to catch up on some deadlines, but mainly to avoid the horrors of the plague. Jonson, as in the bad plague year of 1609 when he was working on his new play, *Epicoene, or The Silent Woman*, remained in London.

The threat of the plague apart, the year found Jonson almost at the meridian of his fortunes. In favour at court, he yet owed that favour to no minion perched precariously on fortune's wheel, but to the king himself. As a writer at the centre of his own world of poets and thinkers and tavern talk, he was poised between the popular triumph of *Volpone* a few years previously and the imminent success of *The Alchemist*. Now, there was the new stage play in prospect — and, more important to Jonson, the royal commissions kept on coming.

On 2 February 1609, *The Masque of Queens*, postponed from Christmas owing to ambassadorial squabbles over precedence, had been chosen to open the new Banqueting House at Whitehall. In it, virtually for the first time, Jonson employed the 'anti-masque' — that grotesque or antic counterpoint to the nobility and splendour of the masque proper. Yet even Jonson's choice of witches as the characters of the anti-masque was an oblique compliment to the king, whose study of *Demonology* was thus included among the classic and learned works cited in the handwritten, annotated edition which Jonson proudly prepared at the command of Prince Henry, the young heir to the throne. In *The Masque of Queens*, the witches were duly supplanted by a pretty allegory in praise of virtue and fame, with the queen herself, alias Bel-Anna, among the dancers. The total cost, of over £3,000 — colossal by the standards of the day — was just another strain on James's chronically impoverished exchequer.

Jonson's next entertainment combined elements of what we would call environmental theatre with the Jacobean equivalent of a hypermarket opening. When the king had confiscated Durham House, to the south of the Strand, from the disgraced Raleigh, he had bestowed it upon his hard-working Lord Treasurer, Salisbury — better remembered as Burleigh's son, the wily Robert Cecil. Now, Salisbury used part of the gardens to build the covered shopping precinct which came to be best known as the New Exchange, but was dubbed 'Britain's Burse' by the king on the occasion of its opening in March 1609. Although Jonson's entertainment of that name is no longer extant, the Cecil family archives suggest that the building itself was employed as the 'stage', with a shopkeeper, his apprentice, and a key-keeper as the main characters. Jonson and his designer, the inevitable Inigo Jones, both received £13 6s 8d for their labours, and professional actors were employed — one of them Jonson's special protégé Nathan Field, and all of them present or past members of the company which was to perform *The Silent Woman* later in the same year.

Because of the plague, the closure of the regular theatres meant that Jonson, a notoriously slow worker, could take his time over the writing of this next play, probably while also planning a further royal entertainment. The investiture of the young heir as Prince of Wales (a title he was to enjoy for only two years before his death in 1612) was to be commemorated by 'barriers' — strictly, the fencing which separated the combatants from the spectators at a tournament, but by then synonymous with the event itself. Such leftovers from the chivalric past were already anachronistic, and the 'challenges' sent forth to all the knights of the kingdom by Prince Henry were part of an elaborate allegory, for which he adopted the name of Meliadus, mythical King of Lyonesse.

For his *Speeches at Prince Henry's Barriers*, Jonson sustained the Arthurian motif, in the process celebrating the peace and moderation which supposedly characterised such 'golden ages' as the classical and the Arthurian — an implicit rebuke to the warlike proclivities of the young prince, but entirely to the taste of his father, whose pacifism was rooted as much in policy as in his own timorous personality. The success of the entertainment, which took place early in the New Year of 1610, must have helped to console Jonson for the suppression of *The Silent Woman* a month or so later.

He had, evidently, sought consolation of another kind during the summer of 1609, when he would have been hard at work on the play — and when two children were conceived whose births, the following spring, were both attributed to Ben Jonson. The name, it's true, was not uncommon, but the diminutive forename *was* distinctive — and, at a time when he was confessedly 'given to venery', our Ben had connections with both the parishes concerned. That the two children must have had different mothers points to a personal involvement with women rather different from that of his misogynist males and androgynous females in *The Silent Women* — all of whom, of course, would have had their sexual qualities still further complicated by the reality of being played by a company of young boys.

The Children's Companies

Education in Elizabethan England, however limited its curriculum by modern standards, placed an emphasis on presentational skills which must have provided a contemporary equivalent of assertiveness training. Disputations, in which opponents had to demonstrate their resourcefulness in oratory as applied to issues of philosophical or theological debate, were routine in schools, and formed an integral part of university examinations. They were even offered as royal entertainment to Elizabeth and James on their visits to Oxford and Cambridge — a reminder of the appetite of the age for displays of rhetorical as of theatrical skills, of a kind that might also be relished in the law courts at Westminster, or in an open-air sermon at St. Paul's Cross. So the plays that schoolboys had long presented as part of their regular education contributed as much to their skills in rhetoric as to their fluency in the classical languages they sometimes employed: indeed, the very term 'acting' at first signified the *gestic* component of the performer's art.

Companies of boy players were originally drawn from the choristers of the schools attached to the Chapel Royal and St. Paul's. At first they gave performances only at court and in front of invited audiences: but they assumed a quasi-commercial status once the Children of the Chapel from Windsor had moved into their own 'private' or indoor playhouse — the so-called 'first' Blackfriars. This was in the same year, 1576, as James Burbage built the Theatre in Shoreditch for adult companies: and Sebastian Westcott's Children of Paul's may even have moved into their own theatre within the cathedral precincts a year or so earlier than this.

However, the first Blackfriars Theatre was closed in 1584, and Paul's Boys temporarily ceased playing in 1590 — apparently because of their injudicious involvement in the Martin Marprelate controversy. During the decade or so which saw the consolidation of the major adult companies, the children thus presented no real threat to their elders. But in 1599 a revived Paul's company began playing under Edward Peers, and in 1600 Henry Evans, in partnership with Nathaniel Giles, leased from Richard Burbage the 'second' theatre at Blackfriars for the use of the Children of the Chapel (who in 1603 received royal patronage as the Children of the Queen's Revels). Almost at once, the so-called 'war of the theatres' brought both companies into the public eye, with John Marston's plays for Paul's involved in a satirical ping-pong with Jonson's for the Chapel Children — Dekker joining in after Jonson added him to his targets at the height of the hostilities in 1601.

Whatever the rights and wrongs of the affair (which may even have been a contrived promotional exercise) it was over by 1604, when Jonson and Marston were collaborating on *Eastward Ho!* with George Chapman. This was a Chapel play, which landed the company in trouble and two of its authors in jail for its slighting references to the recently-crowned King James's fellow-Scots: and it was only one among several plays which drew down official displeasure. Eventually, the company lost its royal patronage in 1606 on account of the *Isle of Gulls* affair, described on page xvi — and then they lost their theatre, too, when at last the King's Men were able to take back the lease of the Blackfriars and themselves begin to play indoors. So it was at the nearby Whitefriars Theatre — empty following the collapse of another children's company which had been playing there — that *Epicoene, or The Silent Woman* was first performed.

Although the company now regained its patronage, and was even to perform again at court, their rivals, the Paul's Boys, had already ceased playing. Moreover, some of its own 'boys' were now grown men — Nathan Field being twenty-two when he played in *The Silent Woman* — and within a few more years the children's companies had disappeared from the theatrical scene. But with Webster and Middleton among the dramatists who wrote for them, in addition to Jonson and the others already mentioned, their contribution to the theatrical repertoire of the early Jacobean period was considerable. But on the limited evidence of the plays that have come down to us, we can only guess how their performing style may or may not have differed from that of the adult companies. Thus, their success in the recently-fashionable dramatic mode of satire (following its banning in book form in 1599) may suggest the broader sweep of caricature — or simply reflect the taste of the fashionable private-theatre audiences for plays with a contemporary bite.

Even more a matter for conjecture must be the relationship of the court and its followers, which under James had become strongly homophilic in its tastes, with companies of pert small boys who were often called upon to mimic the more scandalous sexual antics of their elders. In this respect, *The Silent Woman* is in its way almost as convoluted as *As You Like It* or *Twelfth Night*, with its notorious double-bluff of following the expected convention of having a boy playing a woman, only to turn it upside down by discovering him to have been 'really' a boy all along. Its mannish women no less than its 'ingles' and its 'manikins' were also boys, of course, whose undeveloped or precocious sexuality would have lent an edge to its audience's attention — satiric, paedophilic, what you will — inseparable from Jonson's textual emphasis on cross-gendered comic types.

Pleasures and Pains of Old London

An underlying tension in *The Silent Woman* is that between London proper — the square mile within the gates — and the emerging West End, whose umbilical cord, the Strand, connected the city to the court at Whitehall. It is in some narrow alley off the Strand that Morose presumably lodges, since Sir Amorous, who clearly lives close by, is known to do so — so that he may be within hailing distance of the fashionable passers-by.

This is, as Leo Salingar has pointed out, a very odd domicile for a man who professedly hates noise. Just a few of the street cries and entertainments which added to all the daily din are enumerated in the first scene, and the braziers and armourers mentioned were only the loudest of those who lived above their shops. Even at night there was the watchman to disturb the sensitive sleeper, while a more recent intrusion was the clatter of coaches or 'caroches', which were just coming into use as a regular mode of urban transport. And although the clangour of change-ringing, popular with the Jacobean smart set, would have been muted during this plague-time, instead, as Clerimont reminds us, there would have been the incessant tolling of the passing bell, with its constant intimation of mortality.

In the fourth act, Morose conjures up a purgatory of noise, to which he would willingly be sentenced if only he could thereby rid himself of his wife. Its torments duly begin in a belfry, then progress to Westminster Hall (where shopkeepers plied their trade alongside the lawyers), Tower Wharf (where ordinance was kept for the firing of celebratory cannon at every opportunity), Billingsgate (only recently established as a fishmarket, but already a byword for bad language at full blast), and London Bridge, with its close-packed houses and constant transpontine traffic — which is duly joined in imagination by Morose, whose nightmare of self-torture now takes him to Paris Garden, convenient for bull- and bear-baiting, not to mention the brothels and the theatres. Morose declares that he would even be willing to 'sit out a play' to be rid of a wife.

Oddly, 'the fall of a stag' is the only tumultuous occasion on Morose's list which is more often associated with the country-side than with London — though James hunted in Hyde Park if affairs of state prevented him riding further afield, for his love of the chase perhaps exceeded even his pleasure in personable young men. Maybe Morose is here recollecting his own days as a courtier, which the dramatist almost casually reminds us lie in his past. But nothing in Jonson is *entirely* casual, and just as Morose is distancing himself from his days as a courtier, there are others to aspire to its dubious delights — such as Sir

Amorous La Foole, whose family is allegedly of 'ancient origins' though his knighthood goes back barely ten years, to Essex's promiscuous creations in Ireland. Catapulted unexpectedly into wealth by the death of his elder brother, he tells us that he immediately donned a fair gold jerkin in preference to mourning, 'came over in it hither, showed myself to my friends in court and after that went down to my tenants in the country and surveyed my lands, let new leases, took their money, spent it in the eye o' the land here, and now I can take up at my pleasure'. The 'eye o' the land' was, of course, London.

Sir Amorous, in short, like so many of his fellow landowners, no longer dispenses traditional kinds of hospitality and respon-sibility at home, but takes the profits from his estates to spend on the pleasures of the town — cheerfully disregarding the royal injunctions which intermittently ordered such knights back to their shires. The play is replete with this new breed of courtier: not only has the 'mushroom' Sir John Daw evidently purchased his knighthood from King James for hard cash, but so too has Dauphine — much to his uncle's disgust. In this as in other ways, Jonson's sympathies might be expected to lie with a spokesman for an older order: yet here that spokesman is Morose — as in his long soliloquy in the second act, which quivers with contempt for such nouveau-knights as his nephew.

Nor does Jonson spare the characters who flesh out this microcosm of Jacobean London: thus, we are even carefully informed that Mrs. Otter, besides being a kinswoman of La Foole's, was once a 'rich china-woman that the courtiers visited so often' — plying, that is, one of the new-style luxury trades which catered for a London 'society' just beginning to flex its financial muscle. If there is a measure of sympathy for the humours of Captain Otter, who only reluctantly pursues the social pretensions his wife foists on him, this is presumably because the poor man would far rather be on Bankside, enjoying the baiting of the bulls and bears after which he has even named his favourite drinking vessels.

And this, of course, reminds us that cruelty in Jonson's London was a mass spectator sport, whether it took the form of encouraging fighting cocks to tear one another to pieces, of taunting petty offenders in the stocks or capital ones on the gallows, or of visiting Bedlam in fashionable company, as the lady collegiates propose to Epicoene, to have a good laugh at the lunatics. Playhouses often doubled as bear-baiting arenas, and the instinct for cruelty which relished the spectacle of dogs being torn apart by humiliated wild creatures was shared by those same paying customers who enjoyed watching Dauphine exercise his own streak of sadism to the full.

Of Cruelty, Androgyny, and Kings

Dauphine's climactic cruelty to his uncle is entirely in character, and anticipated in a revealing little exchange with Truewit and Clerimont in Act IV, Scene v. Here, as so often, the three young friends get rather niggly with one another — and Truewit is shocked that Dauphine seems ready to accept poor Jack Daw's offer to sacrifice his left arm if it will spare him fighting a duel: 'How! Maim a man forever for a jest? What a conscience hast thou!' 'As good maim his body as his reputation', grumbles Dauphine — but he has to content himself with giving him six good kicks instead. Later, Truewit has to restrain Dauphine from tweaking La Foole's nose off. Now it may be a mite too solemn to elevate these pranks, as some critics have done, into symbolic castrations: but they are, at least, real physical cruelties, and it is Dauphine who is seen to be enjoying their infliction.

Truewit is rather the voyeur, though it's notable that he defends 'force' towards women, which 'is to them an acceptable violence'. And Clerimont's taste is for mental cruelty: it is he who tempts the two gulls into 'revealing' that they have both lain with Epicoene — while their reluctance to repeat the claim before Morose is apparently out of quite genuine concern for his feelings. They are liars, but they are not unkind. 'Is this gentleman-like, sir!', Daw asks Clerimont, and we are reminded of poor Holofernes, humiliated by Berowne and the callow youths of *Love's Labour's Lost*, with his subdued protest, 'This is not generous, not gentle, not humble.' Nor is it: and nor is the behaviour of these young men — who do not even have the excuse that they are trying to impress the ladies.

Indeed, *The Silent Woman* is remarkable for its complete lack of love interest. No more is heard of Clerimont's 'mistress abroad', mentioned by Truewit in the opening scene — in the same breath as his 'ingle at home', the boy whose homosexual favours Clerimont is thus off-handedly assumed to enjoy. And as for Dauphine, he is apparently more embarrassed than flattered when Truewit persuades the collegiate ladies to turn their sexual attentions towards him. Not only is the male fellowship between Dauphine, Truewit, and Clerimont unruffled by female rivalries, but the collegiates, about whom we quickly learn that they 'live from their husbands', also preserve intact a collective identity which is described as 'most masculine or rather hermaphroditical'. Even that 'precious manikin' and 'wind-fucker' Sir Amorous is said to be inseparable from Sir John Daw — while the only married couple still living together rejoices in the name of Otter, a beast emblematic of not being one thing or the other. But if Truewit's praise for the cosmetics which conceal female blemishes in part depends on the distance he thus keeps from physical proximity with them, such a distance is impossible, as Anne Barton points out, for a husband such as Otter. His description of his wife — who 'takes her self asunder' every night 'into some twenty boxes' and then 'is put together again, like a great German clock' — is not only Websterian in its grotesqueness but entirely apt in a play where attitudes to women vary from the cowed to the contemptuous to the camp.

No wonder, then, that Morose has to be humiliated into a declaration of his own impotence — a false declaration, as his earlier determination to beget an heir that night, made in the privileged honesty of a soliloquy, affirms. Indeed, the most sexually alert characters in the play appear to be young boys. At the very beginning, Clerimont's page is described as being thrown on the bed by his master's mistress, as he evidently is by his master besides: and at the very end, Epicoene himself is declared to be 'almost of years, and will make a good visitant within this twelvemonth'. The grownups appear at best disinterested, at worst positively averse to expressions of their own sexuality — of whatever kind.

'Epicoene' for Jonson's audience would not simply have implied effeminacy, but, as its earlier grammatical sense reflects, a *common* gender — or, as the mighty *Oxford English Dictionary* has it, 'partaking of the characteristics of both sexes': in another word, hermaphroditic. Now the original Hermaphroditus, as the scholarly Jonson well knew, was created, according to Ovid, when a lustful nymph fused herself to a timorous male — the impulse to androgny thus being derived from a femininity which has assumed the male 'prerogative' of sexual aggression.

Yet in *The Symposium*, Plato had also used the image of the hermaphrodite — to suggest the essential oneness of the sexes, as reflected in the cheerful bisexuality of Greek gods and goddesses. And the early Christians had even contemplated the idea of an hermaphroditic God, with the separation of an androgynous Adam into man and woman one of the direct causes of the Fall. Although this belief had been declared heretical by the thirteenth century, it was still possible, as Linda Woodbridge reminds us, for Castiglione to claim in *The Courtier*, 'It is read in scripture that God fashioned male and female in his likeness', while Elyot in *The Governor* derived his golden mean, or ideal of behaviour, from a synthesis of supposedly masculine and feminine qualities. So Jacobean attitudes to androgny were a confusing muddle of classical and philosophical precedent, literary typology, rooted sexual prejudice — and an awareness, whether critical or complacent, that their sovereign's court displayed a good few of its qualities. As, of course, did a company of boy players.

The Matter of Women

The Silent Woman was suppressed after its original performance following a complaint from the king's cousin, Lady Arbella Stuart, that it contained an allusion which connected her name with that of the Prince of Moldavia — an imposter who had once deceived the English court, and claimed an engagement to Lady Arbella herself. Among the Prince of Moldavia's other exploits was that in 1606 he had made a dramatic escape from a Turkish prison . . . disguised as a woman. Lady Arbella's preferred suitor was William Seymour: but had the couple's subsequent marriage produced children, the succession of James's own heirs would have been threatened. Later in 1610 she was, accordingly, confined in the Tower — from which she made a successful albeit short-lived escape . . . disguised as a boy.

So inconvenient heirs and transvestite disguises were not only the stuff of comic plays: and nor were matters of androgynous sexuality. The company which presented *The Silent Woman*, previously known as the Children of the Queen's Revels, had actually lost its royal patronage on account of its production three years earlier of a play by John Day called *The Isle of Gulls*. This not only included among its characters a man disguised as a woman, but also, more contentiously, a king with a clear preference for handsome young men over his neglected wife — a relationship uncomfortably reminiscent of the British monarch's with his queen.

For James was bisexual only to the extent necessary to beget heirs to his kingdom, and his dominant homosexuality was expressed more or less openly in his relationships with his successive favourites, Somerset and Buckingham. His court tended to reflect his own sexual preferences: and courtiers in plays of the period are duly portrayed as effeminate in nature and behaviour — as they were also presented in polemical tracts and pamphlets. Thus, when the intermittent pamphlet war over the dignity and status of women reached its height in 1620, it was *Haec Vir*, an effeminate male with courtly characteristics, who confronted *Hic Mulier* — like Jonson's collegiates, speaking for supposedly 'mannish women' — across the booksellers' shelves.

In the same year, the misogynist pamphleteer Joseph Swetnam was made the villain of a play, *Swetnam the Woman-Hater* — in which the anonymous author has a male character don female disguise, and makes Swetnam, like our Morose, even more ridiculous when he duly falls in love with 'her'. The fictionalised Swetnam also falls back on the time-honoured resort of the misogynist, the male-chauvinist joke. When, during a trial scene, 'Silence in the court' is called, he responds: 'Silence? And none but women? That were strange.' Or, as his real-life original had put it in his *Arraignment of Lewd, Idle, Froward, and Unconstant Women* in 1615, 'a woman's chief strength lies in her tongue'. For the misogynists in Jonson's audiences a decade earlier, Epicoene thus *had* to be a boy because no woman could have kept quiet for so long.

The prattling woman, of course, had long held her place alongside the foolish virgin, the shrewish wife, and the wanton widow in a typological parade that goes back to the clerical misogyny of the middle ages. What is remarkable about the late-Elizabethan and Jacobean 'debate' over women is not that such stereotypes should have been perpetuated, but that they were on occasion vigorously challenged. Sometimes this was by women writers — from the pseudonymous Jane Anger's *Protection for Women*, published in 1589, to Constantia Munda's pugnacious rebuke to Swetnam, *The Worming of a Mad Dog*, in 1617 — and sometimes by male defenders, of whom a few verged on asserting the true equality of the sexes, as did Daniel Tuvil in his *A Sanctuary for Ladies* of 1616.

Ironically, however, misogynist writers generally regarded mere garrulousness as less morally reprehensible than the use of the cosmetics which Truewit so eccentrically defends in *The Silent Woman*. For, like a love of fine clothes, 'painting' was a likely symptom of the evils of pride or lechery, or both. But these were considered age-old — whereas the sin of women desiring to appear in male attire was regarded as peculiarly modern. King James himself was reported as objecting to it in 1620, the year of the *Hic Mulier* controversy — but as early as 1606 Dekker was listing women's adoption of masculine fashions among his *Seven Deadly Sins of London*.

Of course, as social historians insist, it is dangerous to try to deduce from pamphlets and plays the everyday attitudes and behaviour of ordinary people. Sometimes formal controversy might be encouraged for a publisher's profit, or, as Francis Utley suggests, misogyny could become a sort of 'very courtly game' — a variant on the disputation, in which both sides recognised that the typology they were employing was merely a form of artistic shorthand (as, indeed, it was for both sexes in the increasingly popular genre of 'character writing'). In *The Silent Woman*, too, male stereotypes are no less ridiculed than female — the relatively new type of the sexual *braggadocio* for instance, as embodied in the characters of Daw and La Foole. But what of the three gallants — and of Dauphine in particular? They carry off no women, still less do they marry any. Are they models for emulation — or further targets for criticism?

Masques and the Married State

I simply do not believe that the three young gallants of *The Silent Woman* are, as Michael Shapiro, for one, confidently asserts, 'coherent images of the way true aristocrats relate to a fallen world' and 'a model for the audience's behaviour in ethics as well as in fashions'. For a start, they *present* no 'coherent images' of behaviour, and — always a sure signal in Jonson — each *talks* as differently from the others as from the remaining characters in the play. They argue with each other, they dissimulate, and their 'ethics' are those of convenience. They are, merely, a 'college' comparable to that of the ladies, bound together by a shared selfishness and sexual fear, while their relationship to the 'fallen world' is one of close involvement in its gossip, greed, and egotism.

Yet it is without apparent irony that Alexander Leggatt, in a recent study of Jonson's works, suggests that there is 'something positive' in the comradeship of these three tricksters, which represents 'a social bond . . . less secure than ideal marriage', but 'much solider than the marriages in this play'. The young men from King James's court would assuredly have agreed, in part in the light of their own sexual preferences — and in part from their knowledge, personal or vicarious, of marriages which, though not often as bizarre or short-lived as that of Morose, were often just as unhappy. Consider the case of that doubly celebrated subject of Jonson's wedding masques: Lady Frances Howard.

As the critic Robert Dutton has pointed out, 'it would be difficult to find more contrasting views of marriage' than those projected on the one hand by *The Silent Woman* and on the other by the masque *Hymenaei* which Jonson wrote to celebrate the marriage of Lady Frances to the Earl of Essex in 1606 — a marriage purely of convenience, intended to heal a political breach between the two families, in which neither bride nor groom was much over fourteen years old. Jonson's masque concluded with a 'débat' in which Truth argued for the married state, Opinion for the single: and Truth, of course, spectacularly prevailed. In *The Silent Woman*, so far from marriage prevailing, anybody who is already married has cause to regret it, and those who are single do not contemplate a condition which Morose even feigns impotence to escape. Ironically, when, seven years after their marriage, Essex and Lady Frances were divorced, it was on the grounds of the Earl's inability to consummate.

By this time, Lady Frances and the king's favourite Robert Carr, soon afterwards Earl of Somerset, were probably already lovers, and Jonson wrote his masque for the Christmas of 1613, *A Challenge at Tilt*, to celebrate their marriage — now, presumably, one based on mutual love. Within two years, Somerset and his countess, their fortunes in decline before the rising star of young George Villiers, later Duke of Buckingham, were under arrest for having poisoned Carr's own one-time favourite, Sir Thomas Overbury, who had bitterly opposed their marriage. The pair were convicted of his murder in 1616, the year in which Jonson published his *Works* in a folio collection: otherwise proud to name the occasion of each of his masques, and to identify the noble dancers who had taken part, he included neither in the folio versions of *Hymenaei* and *A Challenge at Tilt*.

The historian G. P. V. Akrigg, recording the hapless Overbury's distrust of Lady Frances, believes that her picture, as preserved in the National Portrait Gallery, 'helps to explain his view'. 'An amused sensuality lurks about her mouth', he affirms, and 'a cold appraising stare marks the eyes' — while 'the descending curve of her dress takes advantage of contemporary fashion to display her breasts'. He could be describing any pouting page-three pin-up — and in a sense he is. As John Berger has observed, in painting 'women are depicted in a quite different way than men — not because the feminine is different from the masculine, but because the "ideal" spectator is always assumed to be male, and the image of the woman is designed to flatter him'. What Berger says here is interestingly both true and untrue of our play: the spectator *is* assumed to be male: but it is in part Jonson's resolute refusal to flatter him that makes this such a complex and difficult play.

We see the women of this play as conventionally as the image of Lady Frances Howard strikes a modern historian — and when Jonson presents us with ladies less forbidding than the collegiates and more genuine than Epicoene, they are, no less conventionally, the insipid Celia of *Volpone* or the functional Grace Wellborn of *Bartholomew Fair*. Yet if Jonson's 'ideal spectators' here are the courtly males of the private-theatre audience, their counterparts on stage are, if not impotent, curiously deprived, even of such comic potency as Morose displays when, interrupting Mistress Otter's chastisement of her husband in Act IV, he appears (as the lady later reports to Madame Haughty) 'with a huge long naked weapon in both his hands'.

One's unease at the end of *The Silent Women* is not really on Morose's account. He has, in a sense, got what he wants. No: I suspect that primarily we are *embarrassed* on Dauphine's behalf, at the bad taste and strength of hatred he displays. This is, indeed, a breach of decorum in both the twentieth- and the seventeenth-century sense: and to explain it we need to seek the ghost which Jonson may have been exorcising in this play, which makes it so uniquely uncomfortable among his works.

Uncles and Nephews, Fathers and Sons

In a famous essay, Edmund Wilson elided one of the central characters of *The Silent Woman* with his creator to offer us 'Morose Ben Jonson' — 'a constipated writer, well primed with sack'. He was, opined Wilson, an anal erotic: and 'through Morose and through the characters like him' Jonson was thus 'tormenting himself for what is negative and recessive in his nature'. Other critics, less psychoanalytically smug, have, like Jonson's editor L. A. Beaurline, nonetheless been 'troubled' by 'some deep cynicism, some reserve of self-mockery, of loathing and contempt', which 'seems to lie beneath the dazzling surface of the play'. And Anne Barton tantalisingly suggests that 'it may very well be that the ending of *Epicoene* is as unpleasant as it is' because Jonson 'could not help reaching back by way of the avuncular to the paternal' — for, as she points out, 'Jonson could never write coolly about fathers and sons'. Miss Barton leaves it there: but it's a clue worth following up.

Jonson's true father, who died before he was born, became a 'grave minister' who, in the dramatist's own words to Drummond of Hawthornden, 'lost all his estates under Queen Mary', having been cast into prison on account of his protestant faith. Jonson, thrown into jail on a capital charge in 1598, preserved his life by claiming benefit of clergy — and became a Roman Catholic during his imprisonment. It is almost as if, to follow in his father's footsteps in a nation now resolutely protestant, Jonson could only fully do so by betraying his father's faith. He appears to have heartily disliked his stepfather — who took him from school, and set him to his own despised trade of a bricklayer, when young Ben longed to pursue the calling of a scholar. A master craftsman of his company, and apparently a respectable churchgoer, he was no doubt as scandalised by his stepson's association with the players as he was with the charges of recusancy brought against Jonson in 1606. The man now believed to have been that stepfather, Robert Brett, died in 1609 — the year of *The Silent Woman*. Jonson is unlikely to have mourned his passing, though it could well have brought old feelings and grudges back to the surface. A year or so later, for reasons which have always remained obscure, Jonson returned to the Anglican faith.

When, at the turn of the century, Jonson wrote a New Year's epistle to Sir Philip Sidney's daughter, the Countess of Rutland, he concluded by wishing his newly-married patroness 'my best of wishes — may you bear a son'. His own wife had just borne him their third child, Joseph. Of his other children, one young Ben was soon to join his sister, the firstborn Mary, in an infant grave: and a second Ben was to die before the age of two (the practice of christening a newborn after a dead sibling, here suggesting a desperate attempt to perpetuate his father's name, was not uncommon at the time). So Jonson had to seek surrogate sons — just as he had earlier sought surrogate fathers, successively in his schoolmaster Camden and in the Inns of Court intellectual John Hoskyns. For children, such protégés as the boy players Solomon Pavy and Nathan Field were to be succeeded by that whole 'tribe' which assembled around him in his later years — and which was familiarly known as the 'Sons of Ben'.

In *Volpone*, the play that Jonson wrote before *The Silent Woman*, a moral conclusion is brought about not through any cleverness on the part of the virtuous, but because a surrogate father quarrels with his son. In the play which followed, *The Alchemist*, that model of duplicity, Face, survives because *his* surrogate father forgives his prodigal servant and takes him under his wing. And in *Bartholomew Fair*, Jonson risked incurring royal displeasure with his incisive scorn for the trading of orphaned children for cash through the Court of Wards. Whether consciously, as here, or perhaps unconsciously elsewhere, Jonson felt deeply about the obligations of a father towards a son, or of any such quasi-paternal relationship — as it might be, an uncle's towards the child of his widowed sister, of Morose towards Dauphine. Indeed, besides failing to act us a proper guardian to his nephew, Morose has — as he tells us, with characteristic prolixity, twice — never even been a godfather.

On the evidence of Jonson's verse epitaphs, he seems to have reserved the tenderest love of which he was capable for his children, actual and surrogate. Indeed, I suspect that Morose's real sin in his creator's eyes is less that he has denied his nephew money than that he has denied him love. And Jonson was too honest a writer to pardon *that* denial by offering us a neat comic reconciliation. Dauphine retrieves his patrimony, but there is no forgiveness for the crushed Morose — tricked out of love as well as money. Nor is there any girl in prospect for the emotionally crippled nephew, to give him the son who would be presumed to grace their marriage. Morose has killed something in Dauphine — who is, indeed, in many ways closer to his uncle than to his friends: for though he taunts Morose with the noise of others, he makes remarkably little himself. Even at the close of the play, he leaves it to Truewit to expatiate on all the consequences of a plot which, until a few moments earlier, he has kept entirely to himself. For Dauphine, as for his uncle, Truewit's chatter drowns out all reflection, and the rest is — the last word of the play, before the final appeal for the audience's applause — silence.

Bernard Horsfall *Capulet,* **Georgia Slowe** *Juliet,* **Margaret Courtenay** *Nurse,* **Michael Howell** *Paris,*
Linda Spurrier *Lady Capulet,* **Vincent Regan** *Tybalt*

IVAN KYNCL

Romeo and Juliet

Mark Rylance *Romeo*, **Georgia Slowe** *Juliet*

Georgia Slowe *Juliet*, **Mark Rylance** *Romeo*,
Patrick Godfrey *Friar Laurence*

IVAN KYNCL

IVAN KYNCL

David Bradley *Mephostophiles*, **Gerard Murphy** *Faustus*   **Gerard Murphy** *Faustus*, **with the scholars**

THE PROGRAMME

In addition to cast list, biographies and play notes,
the programme you have purchased for this
performance contains the full text of the play.
Please would you bear in mind that following the
text during the performance is very distracting
to the performers especially when you are seated
in rows close to the stage.

Thank you for your help.

The Persons of the Play

MOROSE, *a gentleman that loves no noise*
DAUPHINE EUGENIE, *a knight, his nephew*
CLERIMONT, *a gentleman, his friend*
TRUEWIT, *another friend*
EPICOENE, *the silent woman*
JOHN DAW, *a knight, her servant*
AMOROUS LA FOOLE, *a knight also*
THOMAS OTTER, *a land and sea captain*
CUTBEARD, *a barber*
MUTE, *one of Morose his servants*
MADAME HAUGHTY ⎫
MADAME CENTAURE ⎬ *ladies collegiates*
MISTRESS MAVIS ⎭
MISTRESS TRUST, *the Lady Haughty's woman* ⎫
MISTRESS OTTER, *the Captain's wife* ⎬ *pretenders*
Parson, Pages, Servants, {Musicians} ⎭

The Scene

London

The text used and reproduced here is taken from the edition
prepared by R. V. Holdsworth for the New Mermaids Series
(Ernest Benn Ltd, 1979). In that edition Jonson's own stage
directions were retained but were amplified, although minimally.
All editorial additions are given between braces.

THE PROLOGUE

Truth says, of old the art of making plays
Was to content the people, and their praise
Was to the Poet money, wine, and bays.
But in this age a sect of writers are,
That only for particular likings care
And will taste nothing that is popular.
With such we mingle neither brains nor breasts;
Our wishes, like to those make public feasts,
Are not to please the cook's tastes, but the guests'.
Yet if those cunning palates hither come,
They shall find guests' entreaty and good room;
And though all relish not, sure there will be some
That, when they leave their seats, shall make 'em say,
Who wrote that piece could so have wrote a play,
But that he knew this was the better way.
For to present all custard or all tart
And have no other meats to bear a part,
Or to want bread and salt, were but coarse art.
The Poet prays you, then, with better thought
To sit, and when his cates are all in brought,
Though there be none far-fet, there will dear-bought
Be fit for ladies; some for lords, knights, squires,
Some for your waiting-wench and city-wires,
Some for your men and daughters of Whitefriars.
Nor is it only while you keep your seat
Here that his feast will last, but you shall eat
A week at ord'naries on his broken meat,
If his Muse be true,
Who commends her to you.

Another

Occasioned by some person's impertinent exception.

The ends of all who for the scene do write
Are, or should be, to profit and delight.
And still 't hath been the praise of all best times,
So persons were not touched, to tax the crimes.
Then, in this play which we present tonight,
And make the object of your ear and sight,
On forfeit of yourselves, think nothing true,
Lest so you make the maker to judge you.
For he knows, poet never credit gained
By writing truths, but things like truths well feigned.
If any yet will, with particular sleight
Of application, wrest what he doth write,
And that he meant or him or her will say,
They make a libel which he made a play.

ACT ONE

Scene One

{Enter} Clerimont. He comes out making himself ready, {followed by} Boy.

CLERIMONT.

Ha' you got the song yet perfect I ga' you, boy?

BOY.

Yes, sir.

CLERIMONT.

Let me hear it.

BOY.

You shall, sir, but i' faith let nobody else.

CLERIMONT.

Why, I pray?

BOY.

It will get you the dangerous name of a poet in town, sir, besides me a perfect deal of ill will at the mansion you wot of, whose lady is the argument of it, where now I am the welcom'st thing under a man that comes there.

CLERIMONT.

I think, and above a man too, if the truth were racked out of you.

BOY.

No, faith, I'll confess before, sir. The gentlewomen play with me and throw me o' the bed, and carry me in to my lady, and she kisses me with her oiled face, and puts a peruke o' my head, and asks me an' I will wear her gown, and I say no; and then she hits me a blow o' the ear and calls me innocent, and lets me go.

CLERIMONT.

No marvel if the door be kept shut against your master, when the entrance is so easy to you. Well, sir, you shall go there no more, lest I be fain to seek your voice in my lady's rushes a fortnight hence. Sing, sir.

Boy sings.

{*Enter Truewit.*}

TRUEWIT.

Why, here's the man that can melt away his time, and never feels it! What between his mistress abroad and his ingle at home, high fare, soft lodging, fine clothes, and his fiddle, he thinks the hours ha' no wings or the day no post-horse. Well, sir gallant, were you struck with the plague this minute or condemned to any capital punishment tomorrow, you would begin then to think and value every article o' your time, esteem it at the true rate, and give all for't.

CLERIMONT.

Why, what should a man do?

TRUEWIT.

Why, nothing, or that which, when 'tis done, is as idle. Hearken after the next horse-race, or hunting-match; lay wagers, praise Puppy, or Peppercorn, Whitefoot, Franklin; swear upon Whitemane's party; spend aloud that my lords may hear you; visit my ladies at night and be able to give 'em the character of every bowler or bettor o' the green. These be the things wherein your fashionable men exercise themselves, and I for company.

CLERIMONT.

Nay, if I have thy authority, I'll not leave yet. Come, the other are considerations when we come to have grey heads and weak hams, moist eyes and shrunk members. We'll think on 'em then; then we'll pray and fast.

TRUEWIT.

Ay, and destine only that time of age to goodness which our want of ability will not let us employ in evil?

CLERIMONT.

Why then 'tis time enough.

TRUEWIT.

Yes, as if a man should sleep all the term and think to effect his business the last day. Oh, Clerimont, this time, because it is an incorporeal thing and not subject to sense, we mock ourselves the fineliest out of it, with vanity and misery indeed, not seeking an end of wretchedness, but only changing the matter still.

CLERIMONT.

Nay, thou'lt not leave now –

TRUEWIT.

See but our common disease! With what justice can we complain that great men will not look upon us nor be at leisure to give our affairs such dispatch as we expect, when we will never do it to ourselves, nor hear nor regard ourselves.

CLERIMONT.

Foh, thou hast read Plutarch's *Morals* now, or some such tedious fellow, and it shows so vilely with thee, 'fore God, 'twill spoil thy wit utterly. Talk me of pins, and feathers, and ladies, and rushes, and such things, and leave this stoicity alone till thou mak'st sermons.

TRUEWIT.

Well, sir, if it will not take, I have learned to lose as little of my kindness as I can. I'll do good to no man against his will, certainly. When were you at the college?

CLERIMONT.

What college?

TRUEWIT.

As if you knew not!

CLERIMONT.

No, faith, I came but from court yesterday.

TRUEWIT.

Why, is it not arrived there yet, the news? A new foundation, sir, here i' the town, of ladies that call themselves the Collegiates, an order between courtiers and country madams, that live from their husbands and give entertainment to all the Wits and Braveries o' the time, as they call 'em, cry down or up what they like or dislike in a brain or a fashion with most masculine or rather hermaphroditical authority, and every day gain to their college some new probationer.

CLERIMONT.

Who is the president?

TRUEWIT.

The grave and youthful matron, the Lady Haughty.

CLERIMONT.

A pox of her autumnal face, her pieced beauty! There's no man can be admitted till she be ready nowadays, till she has painted and perfumed and washed and scoured, but the boy here, and him she wipes her oiled lips upon like a sponge. I have made a song, I pray thee hear it, o' the subject.

{*Boy sings.*}

Song

Still to be neat, still to be dressed,
As you were going to a feast;
Still to be powdered, still perfumed:
Lady, it is to be presumed,
Though art's hid causes are not found,
All is not sweet, all is not sound.

Give me a look, give me a face,
That makes simplicity a grace;
Robes loosely flowing, hair as free:

Such sweet neglect more taketh me
Than all th' adulteries of art:
They strike mine eyes, but not my heart.

TRUEWIT.

And I am clearly o' the other side: I love a good dressing before any beauty o' the world. Oh, a woman is then like a delicate garden; nor is there one kind of it: she may vary every hour, take often counsel of her glass and choose the best. If she have good ears, show 'em; good hair, lay it out; good legs, wear short clothes; a good hand, discover it often; practise any art to mend breath, cleanse teeth, repair eyebrows, paint, and profess it.

CLERIMONT.

How! publicly?

TRUEWIT.

The doing of it, not the manner: that must be private. Many things that seem foul i' the doing, do please, done. A lady should indeed study her face when we think she sleeps; nor when the doors are shut should men be inquiring; all is sacred within, then. Is it for us to see their perukes put on, their false teeth, their complexion, their eyebrows, their nails? You see gilders will not work but enclosed. They must not discover how little serves with the help of art to adorn a great deal. How long did the canvas hang afore Aldgate? Were the people suffered to see the city's *Love* and *Charity* while they were rude stone, before they were painted and burnished? No. No more should servants approach their mistresses but when they are complete and finished.

CLERIMONT.

Well said, my Truewit.

TRUEWIT.

And a wise lady will keep a guard always upon the place, that she may do things securely. I once followed a rude fellow into a chamber, where the poor madam, for haste, and troubled, snatched at her peruke to cover her baldness and put it on the wrong way.

CLERIMONT.

Oh prodigy!

TRUEWIT.

And the unconscionable knave held her in compliment an hour, with that reversed face, when I still looked when she should talk from the tother side.

CLERIMONT.

Why, thou shouldst ha' relieved her.

TRUEWIT.

No, faith, I let her alone, as we'll let this argument, if you please, and pass to another. When saw you Dauphine Eugenie?

CLERIMONT.

Not these three days. Shall we go to him this morning? He is very melancholic, I hear.

TRUEWIT.

Sick o' the uncle, is he? I met that stiff piece of formality, his uncle, yesterday, with a huge turban of nightcaps on his head, buckled over his ears.

CLERIMONT.

Oh, that's his custom when he walks abroad. He can endure no noise, man.

TRUEWIT.

So I have heard. But is the disease so ridiculous in him as it is made? They say he has been upon divers treaties with the fishwives and orange-women, and articles propounded between them. Marry, the chimney-sweepers will not be drawn in.

CLERIMONT.

No, nor the broom-men: they stand out stiffly. He cannot endure a costardmonger, he swoons if he hear one.

TRUEWIT.

Methinks a smith should be ominous.

CLERIMONT.

Or any hammerman. A brazier is not suffered to dwell in the parish, nor an armourer. He would have hanged a pewterer's 'prentice once upon a Shrove Tuesday's riot for being o' that trade, when the rest were quit.

TRUEWIT.

A trumpet should fright him terribly, or the hau'boys?

CLERIMONT.

Out of his senses. The waits of the city have a pension of him not to come near that ward. This youth practised on him one night like the bellman, and never left till he had brought him down to the door with a long sword, and there left him flourishing with the air.

BOY.

Why, sir, he hath chosen a street to lie in so narrow at both ends that it will receive no coaches nor carts nor any of these common noises, and therefore we that love him devise to bring him in such as we may, now and then, for his exercise, to breathe him. He would grow resty else in his ease. His virtue would rust without action. I entreated a bearward one day to come down with the dogs of some four parishes that way, and I thank him he did, and cried his games under Master Morose's window till he was sent crying away with his head made a most bleeding spectacle to the multitude. And another time a fencer, marching to his prize, had his drum most tragically run through for taking that street in his way, at my request.

TRUEWIT.

A good wag. How does he for the bells?

CLERIMONT.

Oh, i' the Queen's time he was wont to go out of town every Saturday at ten o'clock or on holiday eves. But now, by reason of the sickness, the perpetuity of ringing has made him devise a room with double walls and treble ceilings, the windows close shut and caulked, and there he lives by candlelight. He turned away a man last week for having a pair of new shoes that creaked, and this fellow waits on him now in tennis-court socks, or slippers soled with wool, and they talk each to other in a trunk. – See who comes here!

ACT ONE

Scene Two

{Enter} Dauphine.

DAUPHINE.

How now! What ail you, sirs? Dumb?

TRUEWIT.

Struck into stone almost, I am here, with tales o' thine uncle! There was never such a prodigy heard of.

DAUPHINE.

I would you would once lose this subject, my masters, for my sake. They are such as you are that have brought me into that predicament I am with him.

TRUEWIT.

How is that?

DAUPHINE.

Marry, that he will disinherit me, no more. He thinks I and my company are authors of all the ridiculous acts and moniments are told of him.

TRUEWIT.

'Slid, I would be the author of more to vex him; that purpose deserves it: it gives thee law of plaguing him. I'll tell thee what I would do. I would make a false almanac, get it printed, and then ha' him drawn out on a coronation day to the Tower-wharf, and kill him with the noise of the ordinance. Disinherit thee! He cannot, man. Art not thou next of blood, and his sister's son?

DAUPHINE.

Ay, but he will thrust me out of it, he vows, and marry.

TRUEWIT.

How! That's a more portent. Can he endure no noise, and will venture on a wife?

CLERIMONT.

Yes. Why, thou art a stranger, it seems, to his best trick yet. He has employed a fellow this half year all over England to hearken him out a dumb woman, be she of any form or any quality, so she be able to bear children. Her silence is dowry enough, he says.

TRUEWIT.

But I trust to God he has found none.

CLERIMONT.

No, but he has heard of one that's lodged i' the next street to him, who is exceedingly soft-spoken, thrifty of her speech, that spends but six words a day. And her he's about now and shall have her.

TRUEWIT.

Is't possible! Who is his agent i' the business?

CLERIMONT.

Marry, a barber, one Cutbeard, an honest fellow, one that tells Dauphine all here.

TRUEWIT.

Why, you oppress me with wonder! A woman, and a barber, and love no noise!

CLERIMONT.

Yes, faith. The fellow trims him silently and has not the knack with his shears or his fingers, and that continence in a barber he thinks so eminent a virtue as it has made him chief of his counsel.

TRUEWIT.

Is the barber to be seen? or the wench?

CLERIMONT.

Yes, that they are.

TRUEWIT.

I pray thee, Dauphine, let's go thither.

DAUPHINE.

I have some business now; I cannot i' faith.

TRUEWIT.

You shall have no business shall make you neglect this, sir. We'll make her talk, believe it; or if she will not, we can give out at least so much as shall interrupt the treaty. We will break it. Thou art bound in conscience, when he suspects thee without cause, to torment him.

DAUPHINE.

Not I, by any means. I'll give no suffrage to't. He shall never ha' that plea against me that I opposed the least fant'sy of his. Let it lie upon my stars to be guilty, I'll be innocent.

TRUEWIT.

Yes, and be poor, and beg; do, innocent, when some groom of his has got him an heir, or this barber, if he himself cannot. Innocent! – I pray thee, Ned, where lies she? Let him be innocent still.

CLERIMONT.

Why, right over against the barber's, in the house where Sir John Daw lies.

TRUEWIT.

You do not mean to confound me!

CLERIMONT.

Why?

TRUEWIT.

Does he that would marry her know so much?

CLERIMONT.

I cannot tell.

TRUEWIT.

'Twere enough of imputation to her, with him.

CLERIMONT.

Why?

TRUEWIT.

The only talking sir i' th' town! Jack Daw! And he teach her not to speak – God b' w' you. I have some business too.

CLERIMONT.

Will you not go thither then?

TRUEWIT.

Not with the danger to meet Daw, for mine ears.

CLERIMONT.

Why? I thought you two had been upon very good terms.

TRUEWIT.

Yes, of keeping distance.

CLERIMONT.

They say he is a very good scholar.

TRUEWIT.

Ay, and he says it first. A pox on him, a fellow that pretends only to learning, buys titles, and nothing else of books in him.

CLERIMONT.

The world reports him to be very learned.

TRUEWIT.

I am sorry the world should so conspire to belie him.

CLERIMONT.

Good faith, I have heard very good things come from him.

TRUEWIT.

You may. There's none so desperately ignorant to deny that: would they were his own. God b' w' you, gentlemen.

{*Exit.*}

CLERIMONT.

This is very abrupt!

ACT ONE

Scene Three

DAUPHINE.

Come, you are a strange open man to tell everything thus.

CLERIMONT.

Why, believe it, Dauphine, Truewit's a very honest fellow.

DAUPHINE.

I think no other, but this frank nature of his is not for secrets.

CLERIMONT.

Nay, then, you are mistaken, Dauphine. I know where he has been well trusted, and discharged the trust very truly and heartily.

DAUPHINE.

I contend not, Ned, but with the fewer a business is carried, it is ever the safer. Now we are alone, if you'll go thither, I am for you.

CLERIMONT.

When were you there?

DAUPHINE.

Last night, and such a *Decameron* of sport fallen out! Boccace never thought of the like. Daw does nothing but court her, and the wrong way. He would lie with her, and praises her modesty; desires that she would talk and be free, and commends her silence in verses, which he reads and swears are the best that ever man made. Then rails at his fortunes, stamps, and mutines why he is not made a councillor and called to affairs of state.

CLERIMONT.

I pray thee, let's go. I would fain partake this. – Some water, boy.

{*Exit Boy.*}

DAUPHINE.

We are invited to dinner together, he and I, by one that came thither to him, Sir La Foole.

CLERIMONT.

Oh, that's a precious manikin!

DAUPHINE.

Do you know him?

CLERIMONT.

Ay, and he will know you too, if e'er he saw you but once, though you should meet him at church in the midst of prayers. He is one of the Braveries, though he be none o' the Wits. He will salute a judge upon the bench and a bishop in the pulpit, a lawyer when he is pleading at the bar, and a lady when she is dancing in a masque, and put her out. He does give plays and suppers, and invites his guests to 'em aloud out of his window as they ride by in coaches. He has a lodging in the Strand for the purpose, or to watch when ladies are gone to the china-houses or the Exchange, that he may meet 'em by chance and give 'em presents, some two or three hundred pounds' worth of toys, to be laughed at. He is never without a spare banquet or sweetmeats in his chamber, for their women to alight at and come up to, for a bait.

DAUPHINE.

Excellent! He was a fine youth last night, but now he is much finer! What is his christian name? I ha' forgot.

{*Enter Boy.*}

CLERIMONT.

Sir Amorous La Foole.

BOY.

The gentleman is here below that owns that name.

CLERIMONT.

'Heart, he's come to invite me to dinner, I hold my life.

DAUPHINE.

Like enough. Pray thee, let's ha' him up.

CLERIMONT.

Boy, marshal him.

BOY.

With a truncheon, sir?

CLERIMONT.

Away, I beseech you. {*Exit Boy.*} – I'll make him tell us his pedigree now, and what meat he has to dinner, and who are his guests, and the whole course of his fortunes, with a breath.

ACT ONE

Scene Four

{*Enter*} La Foole.

LA FOOLE.

'Save, dear Sir Dauphine, honoured Master Clerimont.

CLERIMONT.

Sir Amorous! You have very much honested my lodging with your presence.

LA FOOLE.

Good faith, it is a fine lodging, almost as delicate a lodging as mine.

CLERIMONT.

Not so, sir.

LA FOOLE.

Excuse me, sir, if it were i' the Strand, I assure you. I am

come, Master Clerimont, to entreat you wait upon two or three ladies to dinner today.

CLERIMONT.

How, sir! Wait upon 'em? Did you ever see me carry dishes?

LA FOOLE.

No, sir, dispense with me; I meant to bear 'em company.

CLERIMONT.

Oh, that I will, sir. The doubtfulness o' your phrase, believe it, sir, would breed you a quarrel once an hour with the terrible boys, if you should but keep 'em fellowship a day.

LA FOOLE.

It should be extremely against my will, sir, if I contested with any man.

CLERIMONT.

I believe it, sir. Where hold you your feast?

LA FOOLE.

At Tom Otter's, sir.

DAUPHINE.

Tom Otter? What's he?

LA FOOLE.

Captain Otter, sir; he is a kind of gamester, but he has had command both by sea and by land.

DAUPHINE.

Oh, then he is *animal amphibium*?

LA FOOLE.

Ay, sir. His wife was the rich china-woman that the courtiers visited so often, that gave the rare entertainment. She commands all at home.

CLERIMONT.

Then she is Captain Otter?

LA FOOLE.

You say very well, sir. She is my kinswoman, a La Foole by the mother side, and will invite any great ladies for my sake.

DAUPHINE.

Not of the La Fooles of Essex?

LA FOOLE.

No, sir, the La Fooles of London.

CLERIMONT.

{*Aside to Dauphine.*} Now h'is in.

LA FOOLE.

They all come out of our house, the La Fooles o' the north, the La Fooles of the west, the La Fooles of the east and south – we are as ancient a family as any is in Europe – but I myself am descended lineally of the French La Fooles – and we do bear for our coat yellow, or or, checkered azure and gules, and some three or four colours more, which is a very noted coat and has sometimes been solemnly worn by divers nobility of our house – but let that go, antiquity is not respected now – I had a brace of fat does sent me, gentlemen, and half a dozen of pheasants, a dozen or two of godwits, and some other fowl, which I would have eaten while they are good, and in good company – there will be a great lady or two, my Lady Haughty, my Lady Centaure, Mistress Dol Mavis – and they come a' purpose to see the silent gentlewoman, Mistress Epicoene, that honest Sir John Daw has promised to bring thither – and then Mistress Trusty, my Lady's woman, will be there too, and this honourable knight, Sir Dauphine, with yourself, Master Clerimont – and we'll be very merry and have fiddlers and dance – I have been a mad wag in my time, and have spent some crowns since I was a page in court to my Lord Lofty, and after my Lady's gentleman-usher, who got me knighted in Ireland, since it pleased my elder brother to die – I had as fair a gold jerkin on that day as any was worn in the Island Voyage or at Caliz, none dispraised, and I came over in it hither, showed myself to my friends in court and after went down to my tenants in the country and surveyed my lands, let new leases, took their money, spent it in the eye o' the land here, upon ladies – and now I can take up at my pleasure.

DAUPHINE.

Can you take up ladies, sir?

CLERIMONT.

Oh, let him breathe, he has not recovered.

DAUPHINE.

Would I were your half in that commodity –

LA FOOLE.

No, sir, excuse me: I meant money, which can take up anything. I have another guest or two to invite and say as much to, gentlemen. I'll take my leave abruptly, in hope you will not fail – Your servant.

{Exit La Foole.}

DAUPHINE.

We will not fail you, sir precious La Foole; but she shall that your ladies come to see, if I have credit afore Sir Daw.

CLERIMONT.

Did you ever hear such a wind-fucker as this?

DAUPHINE.

Or such a rook as the other, that will betray his mistress to be seen! Come, 'tis time we prevented it.

CLERIMONT.

Go.

{Exeunt.}

ACT TWO

Scene One

{*Enter*} *Morose, Mute.*

MOROSE.

Cannot I yet find out a more compendious method than by this trunk to save my servants the labour of speech and mine ears the discord of sounds? Let me see. All discourses but mine own afflict me, they seem harsh, impertinent, and irksome. Is it not possible that thou shouldst answer me by signs, and I apprehend thee, fellow? Speak not, though I question you. You have taken the ring off from the street door, as I bade you? Answer me not by speech but by silence, unless it be otherwise. – Very good.

At the breaches, still the fellow makes legs or signs.

And you have fastened on a thick quilt or flock-bed on the outside of the door, that if they knock with their daggers or with brickbats, they can make no noise? But with your leg, your answer, unless it be otherwise. – Very good. This is not only fit modesty in a servant, but good state and discretion in a master. And you have been with Cutbeard, the barber, to have him come to me? – Good. And he will come presently? Answer me not but with your leg, unless it be otherwise; if it be otherwise, shake your head or shrug. – {*Mute makes a leg.*} So. Your Italian and Spaniard are wise in these, and it is a frugal and comely gravity. How long will it be ere Cutbeard come? Stay, if an hour, hold up your whole hand; if half an hour, two fingers; if a quarter, one. – {*Mute holds up one finger bent.*} Good; half a quarter? 'Tis well. And have you given him a key to come in without knocking? – Good. And is the lock oiled, and the hinges, today? – Good. And the quilting of the stairs nowhere worn out and bare? – Very good. I see by much doctrine and impulsion, it may be effected. Stand by. The Turk in this divine discipline is admirable, exceeding all the potentates of the earth; still waited on by mutes, and all his commands so executed, yea, even in the war, as I have heard, and in his marches, most of his charges and directions given by signs and with silence: an exquisite art! And I am heartily ashamed and angry oftentimes that the princes of Christendom should suffer a barbarian to transcend 'em in so high a point of felicity. I will practise it hereafter.

One winds a horn without.

How now? Oh! oh! What villain, what prodigy of mankind is that? – Look. {*Exit Mute. Horn sounds*} *again.* – Oh! cut his throat, cut his throat! What murderer, hell-hound, devil can this be?

{*Enter Mute.*}

MUTE.

It is a post from the court –

MOROSE.

Out, rogue! And must thou blow thy horn too?

MUTE.

Alas, it is a post from the court, sir, that says he must speak with you, pain of death –

MOROSE.

Pain of thy life, be silent!

ACT TWO

Scene Two

{*Enter*} *Truewit* {*carrying a post-horn and a halter*}.

TRUEWIT.

By your leave, sir – I am a stranger here – is your name Master Morose? – {*To Mute.*} Is your name Master Morose? Fishes, Pythagoreans all! This is strange! What say you, sir? Nothing? Has Harpocrates been here with his club among you? – Well, sir, I will believe you to be the man at this time; I will venture upon you, sir. Your friends at court commend 'em to you, sir –

MOROSE.

{*Aside*}. Oh men! Oh manners! Was there ever such an impudence?

TRUEWIT.

And are extremely solicitous for you, sir.

MOROSE.

Whose knave are you?

TRUEWIT.

Mine own knave and your compeer, sir.

MOROSE.

Fetch me my sword –

TRUEWIT.

You shall taste the one half of my dagger if you do, groom,

and you the other if you stir, sir. Be patient, I charge you in the King's name, and hear me without insurrection. They say you are to marry? To marry! Do you mark, sir?

MOROSE.
How then, rude companion!

TRUEWIT.
Marry, your friends do wonder, sir, the Thames being so near, wherein you may drown so handsomely; or London Bridge at a low fall with a fine leap, to hurry you down the stream; or such a delicate steeple i' the town as Bow, to vault from; or a braver height as Paul's; or if you affected to do it nearer home and a shorter way, an excellent garret window into the street; or a beam in the said garret, with this halter (*He shows him a halter.*), which they have sent, and desire that you would sooner commit your grave head to this knot than to the wedlock noose; or take a little sublimate and go out of the world like a rat, or a fly, as one said, with a straw i' your arse: any way rather than to follow this goblin matrimony. Alas, sir, do you ever think to find a chaste wife in these times? Now? When there are so many masques, plays, Puritan preachings, mad folks, and other strange sights to be seen daily, private and public? If you had lived in King Etheldred's time, sir, or Edward the Confessor's, you might perhaps have found in some cold country hamlet, then, a dull frosty wench would have been contented with one man; now, they will as soon be pleased with one leg or one eye. I'll tell you, sir, the monstrous hazards you shall run with a wife.

MOROSE.
Good sir! Have I ever cozened any friends of yours of their land? bought their possessions? taken forfeit of their mortgage? begged a reversion from 'em? bastarded their issue? What have I done that may deserve this?

TRUEWIT.
Nothing, sir, that I know, but your itch of marriage.

MOROSE.
Why, if I had made an assassinate upon your father, vitiated your mother, ravished your sisters –

TRUEWIT.
I would kill you, sir, I would kill you if you had.

MOROSE.
Why, you do more in this, sir. It were a vengeance centuple for all facinorous acts that could be named, to do that you do –

TRUEWIT.
Alas, sir, I am but a messenger: I but tell you what you must hear. It seems your friends are careful after your soul's health, sir, and would have you know the danger – but you may do your pleasure for them all; I persuade not, sir. If after you are married your wife do run away with a vaulter, or the Frenchman that walks upon ropes, or him that dances the jig, or a fencer for his skill at his weapon, why, it is not their fault; they have discharged their consciences when you know what may happen. Nay, suffer valiantly, sir, for I must tell you all the perils that you are obnoxious to. If she be fair, young, and vegetous, no sweetmeats ever drew more flies; all the yellow doublets and great roses i' the town will be there. If foul and crooked, she'll be with them and buy those doublets and roses, sir. If rich and that you marry her dowry, not her, she'll reign in your house as imperious as a widow. If noble, all her kindred will be your tyrants. If fruitful, as proud as May and humorous as April; she must have her doctors, her midwives, her nurses, her longings every hour, though it be for the dearest morsel of man. If learned, there was never such a parrot; all your patrimony will be too little for the guests that must be invited to hear her speak Latin and Greek, and you must lie with her in those languages too, if you will please her. If precise, you must feast all the silenced brethren once in three days, salute the sisters, entertain the whole family or wood of 'em, and hear long-winded exercises, singings, and catechizings, which you are not given to and yet must give for, to please the zealous matron your wife, who for the holy cause will cozen you over and above. You begin to sweat, sir? But this is not half, i' faith; you may do your pleasure notwithstanding, as I said before; I come not to persuade you. –

The Mute is stealing away.

Upon my faith, master servingman, if you do stir, I will beat you.

MOROSE.
Oh, what is my sin, what is my sin?

TRUEWIT.
Then, if you love your wife, or rather dote on her, sir, oh, how she'll torture you and take pleasure i' your torments! You shall lie with her but when she lists; she will not hurt her beauty, her complexion; or it must be for that jewel or that pearl when she does; every half hour's pleasure must be bought anew, and with the same pain and charge you wooed her at first. Then you must keep what servants she please, what company she will; that friend must not visit you without her license; and him she loves most she will seem to hate eagerliest, to decline your jealousy; or feign to be jealous of you first, and for that cause go live with her she-friend or cousin at the college, that can instruct her in all the mysteries of writing

letters, corrupting servants, taming spies; where she must have that rich gown for such a great day, a new one for the next, a richer for the third; be served in silver; have the chamber filled with a succession of grooms, footmen, ushers, and other messengers, besides embroiderers, jewellers, tire-women, sempsters, feathermen, perfumers; while she feels not how the land drops away, nor the acres melt, nor foresees the change when the mercer has your woods for her velvets; never weighs what her pride costs, sir, so she may kiss a page or a smooth chin that has the despair of a beard; be a stateswoman, know all the news; what was done at Salisbury, what at the Bath, what at court, what in progress; or so she may censure poets and authors and styles, and compare 'em, Daniel with Spenser, Jonson with the tother youth, and so forth; or be thought cunning in controversies or the very knots of divinity, and have often in her mouth the state of the question, and then skip to the mathematics and demonstration, and answer in religion to one, in state to another, in bawdry to a third.

MOROSE.

Oh, oh!

TRUEWIT.

All this is very true, sir. And then her going in disguise to that conjuror and this cunning woman, where the first question is, how soon you shall die? next, if her present servant love her? next that, if she shall have a new servant? and how many? which of her family would make the best bawd, male or female? what precedence she shall have by her next match? And sets down the answers, and believes 'em above the scriptures. Nay, perhaps she'll study the art.

MOROSE.

Gentle sir, ha' you done? Ha' you had your pleasure o' me? I'll think of these things.

TRUEWIT.

Yes, sir; and then comes reeking home of vapour and sweat with going afoot, and lies in a month of a new face, all oil and birdlime, and rises in asses' milk, and is cleansed with a new fucus. God b' w' you, sir. One thing more, which I had almost forgot. This too, with whom you are to marry may have made a conveyance of her virginity aforehand, as your wise widows do of their states, before they marry, in trust to some friend, sir. Who can tell? Or if she have not done it yet, she may do, upon the wedding day, or the night before, and antedate you cuckold. The like has been heard of in nature. 'Tis no devised, impossible thing, sir. God b' w' you. I'll be bold to leave this rope with you, sir, for a remembrance. – Farewell, Mute.

{*Exit.*}

MOROSE.

Come, ha' me to my chamber, but first shut the door.

The horn again.

Oh, shut the door, shut the door. Is he come again?

{*Enter Cutbeard.*}

CUTBEARD.

'Tis I, sir, your barber.

MOROSE.

Oh, Cutbeard, Cutbeard, Cutbeard! here has been a cutthroat with me: help me in to my bed, and give me physic with thy counsel.

{*Exeunt.*}

ACT TWO

Scene Three

{*Enter*} *Daw, Clerimont, Dauphine, Epicoene.*

DAW.

Nay, and she will, let her refuse at her own charges; 'tis nothing to me, gentlemen. But she will not be invited to the like feasts or guests every day.

CLERIMONT.

Oh, by no means, she may not refuse – (*They dissuade her privately.*) to stay at home if you love your reputation. 'Slight, you are invited thither o' purpose to be seen and laughed at by the lady of the college and her shadows. This trumpeter hath proclaimed you.

DAUPHINE.

You shall not go; let him be laughed at in your stead, for not bringing you, and put him to his extemporal faculty of fooling and talking loud to satisfy the company.

CLERIMONT.

He will suspect us, talk aloud. – Pray, Mistress Epicoene, let's see your verses; we have Sir John Daw's leave; do not conceal your servant's merit and your own glories.

EPICOENE.

They'll prove my servant's glories if you have his leave so soon.

DAUPHINE.

{*Aside to Epicoene*}. His vainglories, lady!

DAW.

Show 'em, show 'em, mistress, I dare own 'em.

EPICOENE.

Judge you what glories!

DAW.

Nay, I'll read 'em myself too: an author must recite his own works. It is a madrigal of modesty.
'Modest and fair, for fair and good are near
Neighbours, howe'er' –

DAUPHINE.

Very good.

CLERIMONT.

Ay, is't not?

DAW.

'No noble virtue ever was alone,
But two in one.'

DAUPHINE.

Excellent!

CLERIMONT.

That again, I pray, Sir John.

DAUPHINE.

It has something in't like rare wit and sense.

CLERIMONT.

Peace.

DAW.

'No noble virtue ever was alone,
But two in one.
Then, when I praise sweet modesty, I praise
Bright beauty's rays:
And having praised both beauty' and modestee,
I have praised thee.'

DAUPHINE.

Admirable!

CLERIMONT.

How it chimes, and cries tink i' the close, divinely!

DAUPHINE.

Ay, 'tis Seneca.

CLERIMONT.

No, I think 'tis Plutarch.

DAW.

The dor on Plutarch, and Seneca, I hate it: they are mine own imaginations, by that light. I wonder those fellows have such credit with gentlemen!

CLERIMONT.

They are very grave authors.

DAW.

Grave asses! Mere essayists! A few loose sentences, and that's all. A man would talk so his whole age; I do utter as good things every hour, if they were collected and observed, as either of 'em.

DAUPHINE.

Indeed, Sir John!

CLERIMONT.

He must needs, living among the Wits and Braveries too.

DAUPHINE.

Ay, and being president of 'em as he is.

DAW.

There's Aristotle, a mere commonplace fellow; Plato, a discourser; Thucydides and Livy, tedious and dry; Tacitus, an entire knot, sometimes worth the untying, very seldom.

CLERIMONT.

What do you think of the poets, Sir John?

DAW.

Not worthy to be named for authors. Homer, an old, tedious, prolix ass, talks of curriers and chines of beef; Virgil, of dunging of land and bees; Horace, of I know not what.

CLERIMONT.

I think so.

DAW.

And so Pindarus, Lycophron, Anacreon, Catullus, Seneca the tragedian, Lucan, Propertius, Tibullus, Martial, Juvenal, Ausonious, Statius, Politian, Valerius Flaccus, and the rest –

CLERIMONT.

What a sackful of their names he has got!

DAUPHINE.

And how he pours 'em out! Politian with Valerius Flaccus!

CLERIMONT.

Was not the character right of him?

DAUPHINE.
As could be made, i' faith.

DAW.
And Persius, a crabbed coxcomb not to be endured.

DAUPHINE.
Why, whom do you account for authors, Sir John Daw?

DAW.
Syntagma juris civilis, Corpus juris civilis, Corpus juris canonici, the King of Spain's Bible.

DAUPHINE.
Is the King of Spain's Bible an author?

CLERIMONT.
Yes, and *Syntagma.*

DAUPHINE.
What was that *Syntagma,* sir?

DAW.
A civil lawyer, a Spaniard.

DAUPHINE.
Sure, *Corpus* was a Dutchman.

CLERIMONT.
Ay, both the Corpuses, I knew 'em: they were very corpulent authors.

DAW.
And then there's Vatablus, Pomponatius, Symancha; the other are not to be received within the thought of a scholar.

DAUPHINE.
'Fore God, you have a simple learned servant, lady, in titles.

CLERIMONT.
I wonder that he is not called to the helm and made a councillor!

DAUPHINE.
He is one extraordinary.

CLERIMONT.
Nay, but in ordinary! To say truth, the state wants such.

DAUPHINE.
Why, that will follow.

CLERIMONT.
I muse a mistress can be so silent to the dotes of such a servant.

DAW.
'Tis her virtue, sir. I have written somewhat of her silence too.

DAUPHINE.
In verse, Sir John?

CLERIMONT.
What else?

DAUPHINE.
Why, how can you justify your own being of a poet, that so slight all the old poets?

DAW.
Why, every man that writes in verse is not a poet; you have of the Wits that write verses and yet are no poets: they are poets that live by it, the poor fellows that live by it.

DAUPHINE.
Why, would not you live by your verses, Sir John?

CLERIMONT.
No, 'twere pity he should. A knight live by his verses? He did not make 'em to that end, I hope.

DAUPHINE.
And yet the noble Sidney lives by his, and the noble family not ashamed.

CLERIMONT.
Ay, he professed himself; but Sir John Daw has more caution: he'll not hinder his own rising i' the state so much! Do you think he will? Your verses, good Sir John, and no poems.

DAW.
'Silence in woman is like speech in man,
Deny't who can.'

DAUPHINE.
Not I, believe it; your reason, sir.

DAW.
'Nor is't a tale
That female vice should be a virtue male,
Or masculine vice, a female virtue be:
You shall it see
Proved with increase,
I know to speak, and she to hold her peace.'
Do you conceive me, gentlemen?

DAUPHINE.
No, faith; how mean you 'with increase', Sir John?

DAW.

Why, 'with increase' is when I court her for the common cause of mankind, and she says nothing, but *consentire videtur*, and in time is *gravida*.

DAUPHINE.

Then this is a ballad of procreation?

CLERIMONT.

A madrigal of procreation; you mistake.

EPICOENE.

Pray give me my verses again, servant.

DAW..

If you'll ask 'em aloud, you shall.

{*Walks apart with Epicoene.*}

CLERIMONT.

See, here's Truewit again!

ACT TWO

Scene Four

{*Enter*} Truewit {*with his post-horn*}.

CLERIMONT.

Where has thou been, in the name of madness, thus accoutred with thy horn?

TRUEWIT.

Where the sound of it might have pierced your senses with gladness had you been in ear-reach of it. Dauphine, fall down and worship me: I have forbid the banns, lad. I have been with thy virtuous uncle and have broke the match.

DAUPHINE.

You ha' not, I hope.

TRUEWIT.

Yes, faith; and thou shouldst hope otherwise, I should repent me. This horn got me entrance, kiss it. I had no other way to get in but by feigning to be a post; but when I got in once, I proved none, but rather the contrary, turned him into a post or a stone or what is stiffer, with thund'ring into him the incommodities of a wife and the miseries of marriage. If ever Gorgon were seen in the shape of a woman, he hath seen her in my description. I have put him off o' that scent forever.

Why do you not applaud and adore me, sirs? Why stand you mute? Are you stupid? You are not worthy o' the benefit.

DAUPHINE.

Did not I tell you? mischief! –

CLERIMONT.

I would you had placed this benefit somewhere else.

TRUEWIT.

Why so?

CLERIMONT.

'Slight, you have done the most inconsiderate, rash, weak thing that ever man did to his friend.

DAUPHINE.

Friend! If the most malicious enemy I have had studied to inflict an injury upon me, it could not be a greater.

TRUEWIT.

Wherein, for God's sake? Gentlemen, come to yourselves again.

DAUPHINE.

But I presaged thus much afore to you.

CLERIMONT.

Would my lips had been soldered when I spake on't. 'Slight, what moved you to be thus impertinent?

TRUEWIT.

My masters, do not put on this strange face to pay my courtesy; off with this visor. Have good turns done you and thank 'em this way?

DAUPHINE.

'Fore heav'n, you have undone me. That which I have plotted for and been maturing now these four months, you have blasted in a minute. Now I am lost, I may speak. This gentlewoman was lodged here by me o' purpose, and, to be put upon my uncle, hath professed this obstinate silence for my sake, being my entire friend, and one that for the requital of such a fortune as to marry him, would have made me very ample conditions; where now all my hopes are utterly miscarried by this unlucky accident.

CLERIMONT.

Thus 'tis when a man will be ignorantly officious, do services and not know his why. I wonder what courteous itch possessed you! You never did absurder part i' your life, nor a greater trespass to friendship, to humanity.

DAUPHINE.

Faith, you may forgive it best; 'twas your cause principally.

CLERIMONT.

I know it; would it had not.

{*Enter Cutbeard.*}

DAUPHINE.

How now, Cutbeard, what news?

CUTBEARD.

The best, the happiest that ever was, sir. There has been a mad gentleman with your uncle this morning – {*Seeing Truewit.*} I think this be the gentleman – that has almost talked him out of his wits with threat'ning him from marriage –

DAUPHINE.

On, I pray thee.

CUTBEARD.

And your uncle, sir, he thinks 'twas done by your procurement; therefore he will see the party you wot of presently, and if he like her, he says, and that she be so inclining to dumb as I have told him, he swears he will marry her today, instantly, and not defer it a minute longer.

DAUPHINE.

Excellent! Beyond our expectation!

TRUEWIT.

Beyond your expectation? By this light, I knew it would be thus.

DAUPHINE.

Nay, sweet Truewit, forgive me.

TRUEWIT.

No, I was 'ignorantly officious, impertinent'; this was the 'absurb, weak part.'

CLERIMONT.

Wilt thou ascribe that to merit now, was mere fortune?

TRUEWIT.

Fortune? Mere providence. Fortune had not a finger in't. I saw it must necessarily in nature fall out so: my genius is never false to me in these things. Show me how it could be otherwise.

DAUPHINE.

Nay, gentlemen, contend not; 'tis well now.

TRUEWIT.

Alas, I let him go on with 'inconsiderate', and 'rash', and what he pleased.

CLERIMONT.

Away, thou strange justifier of thyself, to be wiser than thou wert by the event.

TRUEWIT.

Event! By this light, thou shalt never persuade me but I foresaw it as well as the stars themselves.

DAUPHINE.

Nay, gentlemen, 'tis well now. Do you two entertain Sir John Daw with discourse while I send her away with instructions.

TRUEWIT.

I'll be acquainted with her first, by your favour.

{*They approach Epicoene and Daw.*}

CLERIMONT.

Master Truewit, lady, a friend of ours.

TRUEWIT.

I am sorry I have not known you sooner, lady, to celebrate this rare virtue of your silence.

CLERIMONT.

Faith, an' you had come sooner, you should ha' seen and heard her well celebrated in Sir John Daw's madrigals.

{*Exeunt Dauphine, Epicoene, and Cutbeard.*}

TRUEWIT.

Jack Daw, God save you, when saw you La Foole?

DAW.

Not since last night, Master Truewit.

TRUEWIT.

That's miracle! I thought you two had been inseparable.

DAW.

He's gone to invite his guests.

TRUEWIT.

Gods so, 'tis true! What a false memory have I towards that man! I am one: I met him e'en now upon that he calls his delicate fine black horse, rid into a foam with posting from place to place and person to person to give 'em the cue –

CLERIMONT.

Lest they should forget?

TRUEWIT.

Yes; there was never poor captain took more pains at a muster to show men than he at this meal to show friends.

DAW.

It is his quarter-feast, sir.

CLERIMONT.

What, do you say so, Sir John?

TRUEWIT.

Nay, Jack Daw will not be out, at the best friends he has, to the talent of his wit. Where's his mistress, to hear and applaud him? Is she gone?

DAW.

Is Mistress Epicoene gone?

CLERIMONT.

Gone afore with Sir Dauphine, I warrant, to the place.

TRUEWIT.

Gone afore! That were a manifest injury, a disgrace and a half, to refuse him at such a festival time as this, being a Bravery and a Wit too.

CLERIMONT.

Tut, he'll swallow it like cream: he's better read in *jure civili* than to esteem anything a disgrace is offered him from a mistress.

DAW.

Nay, let her e'en go; she shall sit alone and be dumb in her chamber a week together, for Sir John Daw, I warrant her. Does she refuse me?

CLERIMONT.

No, sir, do not take it so to heart: she does not refuse you, but a little neglect you. Good faith, Truewit, you were too blame to put it into his head that she does refuse him.

TRUEWIT.

She does refuse him, sir, palpably, however you mince it. An' I were as he, I would swear to speak ne'er a word to her today for't.

DAW.

By this light, no more I will not.

TRUEWIT.

Nor to anybody else, sir.

DAW.

Nay, I will not say so, gentlemen.

CLERIMONT.

It had been an excellent happy condition for the company if you could have drawn him to it.

DAW.

I'll be very melancholic, i' faith.

CLERIMONT.

As a dog, if I were as you, Sir John.

TRUEWIT.

Or a snail or a hog-louse: I would roll myself up for this day; in troth, they should not unwind me.

DAW.

By this picktooth, so I will.

CLERIMONT.

'Tis well done: he begins already to be angry with his teeth.

DAW.

Will you go, gentlemen?

CLERIMONT.

Nay, you must walk alone if you be right melancholic, Sir John.

TRUEWIT.

Yes, sir, we'll dog you, we'll follow you afar off.

{*Exit Daw.*}

CLERIMONT.

Was there ever such a two yards of knighthood, measured out by time, to be sold to laughter?

TRUEWIT.

A mere talking mole! Hang him, no mushroom was ever so fresh. A fellow so utterly nothing, as he knows not what he would be.

CLERIMONT.

Let's follow him, but first let's go to Dauphine; he's hovering about the house to hear what news.

TRUEWIT.

Content.

{*Exeunt.*}

ACT TWO

Scene Five

{*Enter*} *Morose, Epicoene, Cutbeard, Mute.*

MOROSE.

Welcome, Cutbeard; draw near with your fair charge, and in

her ear softly entreat her to unmask. {*Cutbeard whispers to Epicoene, who removes her mask.*} So. Is the door shut? – {*Mute makes a leg.*} Enough. Now, Cutbeard, with the same discipline I use to my family, I will question you. As I conceive, Cutbeard, this gentlewoman is she you have provided and brought, in hope she will fit me in the place and person of a wife? Answer me not but with your leg, unless it be otherwise. – Very well done, Cutbeard. I conceive besides, Cutbeard, you have been pre-acquainted with her birth, education, and qualities, or else you would not prefer her to my acceptance, in the weighty consequence of marriage. – This I conceive, Cutbeard. Answer me not but with your leg, unless it be otherwise. – Very well done, Cutbeard. Give aside now a little, and leave me to examine her condition and aptitude to my affection. (*He goes about her and views her.*) She is exceeding fair and of a special good favour; a sweet composition or harmony of limbs; her temper of beauty has the true height of my blood. The knave hath exceedingly well fitted me without: I will now try her within. – Come near, fair gentlewoman; let not my behaviour seem rude, though unto you, being rare, it may haply appear strange. (*She curtsies.*) Nay, lady, you may speak, though Cutbeard and my man might not: for of all sounds only the sweet voice of a fair lady has the just length of mine ears. I beseech you, say, lady; out of the first fire of meeting eyes, they say, love is stricken: do you feel any such motion suddenly shot into you from any part you see in me? Ha, lady? (*Curtsy.*) Alas, lady, these answers by silent curtsies from you are too courtless and simple. I have ever had my breeding in court, and she that shall be my wife must be accomplished with courtly and audacious ornaments. Can you speak, lady?

EPICOENE.
Judge you, forsooth.

She speaks softly.

MOROSE.
What say you, lady? Speak out, I beseech you.

EPICOENE.
Judge you, forsooth.

MOROSE.
O' my judgement, a divine softness! But can you naturally, lady, as I enjoin these by doctrine and industry, refer yourself to the search of my judgement and, not taking pleasure in your tongue, which is a woman's chiefest pleasure, think it plausible to answer me by silent gestures, so long as my speeches jump right with what you conceive? (*Curtsy.*) Excellent! Divine! If it were possible she should hold out

thus! Peace, Cutbeard, thou art made forever, as thou hast made me, if this felicity have lasting; but I will try her further. Dear lady, I am courtly, I tell you, and I must have mine ears banqueted with pleasant and witty conferences, pretty girds, scoffs, and dalliance in her that I mean to choose for my bed-fere. The ladies in court think it a most desperate impair to their quickness of wit and good carriage if they cannot give occasion for a man to court 'em, and when an amorous discourse is set on foot, minister as good matter to continue it as himself; and do you alone so much differ from all them that what they, with so much circumstance, affect and toil for, to seem learned, to seem judicious, to seem sharp and conceited, you can bury in yourself with silence, and rather trust your graces to the fair conscience of virtue than to the world's or your own proclamation?

EPICOENE.
I should be sorry else.

MOROSE.
What say you, lady? Good lady, speak out.

EPICOENE.
I should be sorry, else.

MOROSE.
That sorrow doth fill me with gladness! Oh, Morose, thou art happy above mankind! Pray that thou mayst contain thyself. I will only put her to it once more, and it shall be with the utmost touch and test of their sex. – But hear me, fair lady; I do also love to see her whom I shall choose for my heifer to be the first and principal in all fashions, precede all the dames at court by a fortnight, have her council of tailors, lineners, lace-women, embroiderers, and sit with 'em sometimes twice a day upon French intelligences, and then come forth varied like Nature, or oft'ner than she, and better by the help of Art, her emulous servant. This do I affect. And how will you be able, lady, with this frugality of speech, to give the manifold, but necessary, instructions for that bodice, these sleeves, those skirts, this cut, that stitch, this embroidery, that lace, this wire, those knots, that ruff, those roses, this girdle, that fan, the tother scarf, these gloves? Ha? What say you, lady?

EPICOENE.
I'll leave it to you, sir.

MOROSE.
How, lady? Pray you, rise a note.

EPICOENE.
I leave it to wisdom and you, sir.

MOROSE.

Admirable creature! I will trouble you no more; I will not sin against so sweet a simplicity. Let me now be bold to print on those divine lips the seal of being mine. {*Kisses her.*} Cutbeard, I give thee the lease of thy house free; thank me not, but with thy leg. – I know what thou wouldst say, she's poor and her friends deceased: she has brought a wealthy dowry in her silence, Cutbeard, and in respect of her poverty, Cutbeard, I shall have her more loving and obedient, Cutbeard. Go thy ways and get me a minister presently, with a soft, low voice, to marry us, and pray him he will not be impertinent, but brief as he can; away; softly, Cutbeard. {*Exit Cutbeard.*} Sirrah, conduct your mistress into the dining room, your now-mistress. {*Exeunt Mute and Epicoene.*} Oh my felicity! How I shall be revenged on mine insolent kinsman and his plots to fright me from marrying! This night I will get an heir and thrust him out of my blood like a stranger. He would be knighted, forsooth, and thought by that means to reign over me, his title must do it: no, kinsman, I will now make you bring me the tenth lord's and the sixteenth lady's letter, kinsman, and it shall do you no good, kinsman. Your knighthood itself shall come on its knees, and it shall be rejected; it shall be sued for its fees to execution, and not be redeemed; it shall cheat at the twelvepenny ordinary, it knighthood, for its diet all the term time, and tell tales for it in the vacation, to the hostess; or it knighthood shall do worse, take sanctuary in Coleharbour, and fast. It shall fright all it friends with borrowing letters, and when one of the fourscore hath brought it knighthood ten shillings, it knighthood shall go to the Cranes or the Bear at the Bridge-foot and be drunk in fear; it shall not have money to discharge one tavern-reckoning, to invite the old creditors to forbear it knighthood, or the new that should be, to trust it knighthood. It shall be the tenth name in the bond, to take up the commodity of pipkins and stone jugs, and the part thereof shall not furnish it knighthood forth for the attempting of a baker's widow, a brown baker's widow. It shall give it knighthood's name for a stallion to all gamesome citizens' wives, and be refused, when the master of a dancing school or – how do you call him? – the worst reveller in the town is taken; it shall want clothes, and by reason of that, wit, to fool to lawyers. It shall not have hope to repair itself by Constantinople, Ireland, or Virginia; but the best and last fortune to it knighthood shall be to make Dol Tearsheet or Kate Common a lady, and so it knighthood may eat.

{*Exit.*}

ACT TWO

Scene Six

{*Enter*} *Truewit, Dauphine, Clerimont.*

TRUEWIT.

Are you sure he is not gone by?

DAUPHINE.

No, I stayed in the shop ever since.

CLERIMONT.

But he may take the other end of the lane.

DAUPHINE.

No, I told him I would be here at this end; I appointed him hither.

TRUEWIT.

What a barbarian it is to stay then!

{*Enter Cutbeard.*}

DAUPHINE.

Yonder he comes.

CLERIMONT.

And his charge left behind him, which is a very good sign, Dauphine.

DAUPHINE.

How now, Cutbeard, succeeds it or no?

CUTBEARD.

Past imagination, sir, *omnia secunda*; you could not have prayed to have had it so well. *Saltat senex*, as it is i' the proverb; he does triumph in his felicity, admires the party! He has given me the lease of my house too! And I am now going for a silent minister to marry 'em, and away.

TRUEWIT.

'Slight, get one o' the silenced ministers; a zealous brother would torment him purely.

CUTBEARD.

Cum privilegio, sir.

DAUPHINE.

Oh, by no means: let's do nothing to hinder it now; when 'tis done and finished, I am for you, for any device of vexation.

CUTBEARD.

And that shall be within this half hour, upon my dexterity,

gentlemen. Contrive what you can in the meantime, *bonis avibus.*

{Exit.}

CLERIMONT.
How the slave doth Latin it!

TRUEWIT.
It would be made a jest to posterity, sirs, this day's mirth, if ye will.

CLERIMONT.
Beshrew his heart that will not, I pronounce.

DAUPHINE.
And for my part. What is't?

TRUEWIT.
To translate all La Foole's company and his feast hither today, to celebrate this bridal.

DAUPHINE.
Ay, marry, but how will't be done?

TRUEWIT.
I'll undertake the directing of all the lady guests thither, and then the meat must follow.

CLERIMONT.
For God's sake, let's effect it; it will be an excellent comedy of affliction, so many several noises.

DAUPHINE.
But are they not at the other place already, think you?

TRUEWIT.
I'll warrant you for the college-honours: one o' their faces has not the priming colour laid on yet, nor the other her smock sleeked.

CLERIMONT.
Oh, but they'll rise earlier than ordinary to a feast.

TRUEWIT.
Best go see and assure ourselves.

CLERIMONT.
Who knows the house?

TRUEWIT.
I'll lead you. Were you never there yet?

DAUPHINE.
Not I.

CLERIMONT.
Nor I.

TRUEWIT.
Where ha' you lived then? Not know Tom Otter!

CLERIMONT.
No. For God's sake, what is he?

TRUEWIT.
An excellent animal, equal with your Daw or La Foole, if not transcendent, and does Latin it as much as your barber. He is his wife's subject; he calls her princess, and at such times as these follows her up and down the house like a page, with his hat off, partly for heat, partly for reverence. At this instant he is marshalling of his bull, bear and horse.

DAUPHINE.
What be those, in the name of Sphinx?

TRUEWIT.
Why, sir, he has been a great man at the Bear Garden in his time, and from that subtle sport has ta'en the witty denomination of his chief carousing cups. One he calls his bull, another his bear, another his horse. And then he has his lesser glasses, that he calls his deer and his ape, and several degrees of 'em too, and never is well, nor thinks any entertainment perfect, till these be brought out and set o' the cupboard.

CLERIMONT.
For God's love, we should miss this if we should not go!

TRUEWIT.
Nay, he has a thousand things as good that will speak him all day. He will rail on his wife, with certain commonplaces, behind her back, and to her face —

DAUPHINE.
No more of him. Let's go see him, I petition you.

{Exeunt.}

ACT THREE

Scene One

{*Enter*} *Otter, Mistress Otter. Truewit, Clerimont, Dauphine* {*presently follow, unobserved*}.

OTTER.

Nay, good princess, hear me *pauca verba*.

MISTRESS OTTER.

By that light, I'll ha' you chained up with your bull-dogs and bear-dogs, if you be not civil the sooner. I'll send you to kennel, i' faith. You were best bait me with your bull, bear, and horse! Never a time that the courtiers or collegiates come to the house, but you make it a Shrove Tuesday! I would have you get your Whitsuntide velvet cap and your staff i' your hand to entertain 'em; yes, in troth, do.

OTTER.

Not so, princess, neither, but under correction, sweet princess, gi' me leave – these things I am known to the courtiers by. It is reported to them for my humour, and they receive it so, and do expect it. Tom Otter's bull, bear, and horse is known all over England, in *rerum natura*.

MISTRESS OTTER.

'Fore me, I will 'na-ture' 'em over to Paris Garden and 'na-ture' you thither too, if you pronounce 'em again. Is a bear a fit beast, or a bull, to mix in society with great ladies? Think i' your discretion, in any good polity?

OTTER.

The horse then, good princess.

MISTRESS OTTER.

Well, I am contented for the horse; they love to be well horsed, I know. I love it myself.

OTTER.

And it is a delicate fine horse this. *Poetarum Pegasus.* Under correction, princess, Jupiter did turn himself into a – *taurus*, or bull, under correction, good princess.

MISTRESS OTTER.

By my integrity, I'll send you over to the Bankside, I'll commit you to the master of the Garden, if I hear but a syllable more. Must my house, or my roof, be polluted with the scent of bears and bulls, when it is perfumed for great ladies? Is this according to the instrument when I married you? That I would be princess and reign in mine own house, and you would be my subject and obey me? What did you bring me, should make you thus peremptory? Do I allow you your half-crown a day to spend where you will among your gamesters, to vex and torment me at such times as these? Who gives you your maintenance, I pray you? Who allows you your horse-meat and man's meat? Your three suits of apparel a year? Your four pair of stockings, one silk, three worsted? Your clean linen, your bands and cuffs, when I can get you to wear 'em? 'Tis mar'l you ha' 'em on now. Who graces you with courtiers or great personages, to speak to you out of their coaches, and come home to your house? Were you ever so much as looked upon by a lord, or a lady, before I married you, but on the Easter or Whitsun holidays, and then out at the Banqueting House window, when Ned Whiting or George Stone were at the stake?

TRUEWIT.

{*Aside*}. For God's sake, let's go stave her off him.

MISTRESS OTTER.

Answer me to that. And did not I take you up from thence in an old greasy buff-doublet, with points, and green vellet sleeves out at the elbows? You forget this.

TRUEWIT.

{*Aside*}. She'll worry him, if we help not in time.

{*They come forward.*}

MISTRESS OTTER.

Oh, here are some o' the gallants! Go to, behave yourself distinctly, and with good morality, or I protest, I'll take away your exhibition.

ACT THREE

Scene Two

TRUEWIT.

By your leave, fair Mistress Otter, I'll be bold to enter these gentlemen in your acquaintance.

MISTRESS OTTER.

It shall not be obnoxious of difficil, sir.

TRUEWIT.

How does my noble captain? Is the bull, bear, and horse in *rerum natura* still?

OTTER.

Sir, *sic visum superis*.

MISTRESS OTTER.

I would you would but intimate 'em, do. Go your ways in, and get toasts and butter made for the woodcocks. That's a fit province for you.

{*Exit Otter.*}

CLERIMONT.

{*Aside to Truewit and Dauphine*}. Alas, what a tyranny is this poor fellow married to!

TRUEWIT.

Oh, but the sport will be anon, when we get him loose.

DAUPHINE.

Dares he ever speak?

TRUEWIT.

No Anabaptist ever railed with the like license: but mark her language in the meantime, I beseech you.

MISTRESS OTTER.

Gentlemen, you are very aptly come. My cousin, Sir Amorous, will be here briefly.

TRUEWIT.

In good time, lady. Was not Sir John Daw here, to ask for him and the company?

MISTRESS OTTER.

I cannot assure you, Master Truewit. Here was a very melancholy knight in a ruff, that demanded my subject for somebody, a gentleman, I think.

CLERIMONT.

Ay, that was he, lady.

MISTRESS OTTER.

But he departed straight, I can resolve you.

DAUPHINE.

What an excellent choice phrase this lady expresses in!

TRUEWIT.

Oh, sir, she is the only authentical courtier that is not naturally bred one, in the city.

MISTRESS OTTER.

You have taken that report upon trust, gentlemen.

TRUEWIT.

No, I assure you, the court governs it so, lady, in your behalf.

MISTRESS OTTER.

I am the servant of the court and courtiers, sir.

TRUEWIT.

They are rather your idolaters.

MISTRESS OTTER.

Not so, sir.

{*Enter Cutbeard. Dauphine, Truewit and Clerimont converse with him apart.*}

DAUPHINE.

How now, Cutbeard? Any cross?

CUTBEARD.

Oh, no, sir, *omnia bene*. 'Twas never better o' the hinges, all's sure. I have so pleased him with a curate that he's gone to't almost with the delight he hopes for soon.

DAUPHINE.

What is he for a vicar?

CUTBEARD.

One that has catched a cold, sir, and can scarce be heard six inches off, as if he spoke out of a bulrush that were not picked, or his throat were full of pith; a fine quick fellow and an excellent barber of prayers. I came to tell you, sir, that you might *omnem movere lapidem*, as they say, be ready with your vexation.

DAUPHINE.

Gramercy, honest Cutbeard; be thereabouts with thy key to let us in.

CUTBEARD.

I will not fail you, sir: *ad manum*.

{*Exit.*}

TRUEWIT.

Well, I'll go watch my coaches.

CLERIMONT.

Do, and we'll send Daw to you if you meet him not.

{*Exit Truewit.*}

MISTRESS OTTER.

Is Master Truewit gone?

DAUPHINE.

Yes, lady, there is some unfortunate business fallen out.

MISTRESS OTTER.

So I judged by the physiognomy of the fellow that came in, and I had a dream last night too of the new pageant and my

Lady Mayoress, which is always very ominous to me. I told it my Lady Haughty t'other day, when her honour came hither to see some China stuffs, and she expounded it out of Artemidorus, and I have found it since very true. It has done me many affronts.

CLERIMONT.
Your dream, lady?

MISTRESS OTTER.
Yes, sir, anything I do but dream o' the city. It stained me a damask table-cloth, cost me eighteen pound at one time, and burnt me a black satin gown as I stood by the fire at my Lady Centaure's chamber in the college another time. A third time, at the lord's masque, it dropped all my wire and my ruff with wax candle, that I could not go up to the banquet. A fourth time, as I was taking coach to go to Ware to meet a friend, it dashed me a new suit all over – a crimson satin doublet and black velvet skirts – with a brewer's horse, that I was fain to go in and shift me, and kept my chamber a leash of days for the anguish of it.

DAUPHINE.
These were dire mischances, lady.

CLERIMONT.
I would not dwell in the city, and 'twere so fatal to me.

MISTRESS OTTER.
Yes, sir, but I do take advice of my doctor, to dream of it as little as I can.

DAUPHINE.
You do well, Mistress Otter.

{*Enter Daw; Clerimont takes him aside.*}

MISTRESS OTTER.
Will it please you to enter the house farther, gentlemen?

DAUPHINE.
And your favour, lady; but we stay to speak with a knight, Sir John Daw, who is here come. We shall follow you, lady.

MISTRESS OTTER.
At your own time, sir. It is my cousin Sir Amorous his feast –

DAUPHINE.
I know it, lady.

MISTRESS OTTER.
And mine together. But it is for his honour, and therefore I take no name of it, more than of the place.

DAUPHINE.
You are a bounteous kinswoman.

MISTRESS OTTER.
Your servant, sir.

{*Exit.*}

ACT THREE

Scene Three

{*Clerimont comes forward with Daw.*}

CLERIMONT.
Why, do not you know it, Sir John Daw?

DAW.
No, I am a rook if I do.

CLERIMONT.
I'll tell you then: she's married by this time! And whereas you were put i' the head that she was gone with Sir Dauphine, I assure you Sir Dauphine has been the noblest, honestest friend to you that ever gentleman of your quality could boast of. He has discovered the whole plot, and made your mistress so acknowledging and indeed so ashamed of her injury to you, that she desires you to forgive her, and but grace her wedding with your presence today – she is to be married to a very good fortune, she says, his uncle, old Morose; and she willed me in private to tell you that she shall be able to do you more favours, and with more security now than before.

DAW.
Did she say so, i' faith?

CLERIMONT.
Why, what do you think of me, Sir John? Ask Sir Dauphine.

DAW.
Nay, I believe you. Good Sir Dauphine, did she desire me to forgive her?

DAUPHINE.
I assure you, Sir John, she did.

DAW.
Nay, then, I do with all my heart, and I'll be jovial.

CLERIMONT.

Yes, for look you, sir, this was the injury to you. La Foole intended this feast to honour her bridal day, and made you the property to invite the college ladies and promise to bring her; and then at the time she should have appeared, as his friend, to have given you the dor. Whereas now, Sir Dauphine has brought her to a feeling of it, with this kind of satisfaction, that you shall bring all the ladies to the place where she is, and be very jovial; and there she will have a dinner which shall be in your name, and so disappoint La Foole, to make you good again and, as it were, a saver i' the man.

DAW.

As I am a knight, I honour her and forgive her heartily.

CLERIMONT.

About it then presently. Truewit is gone before to confront the coaches, and to acquaint you with so much if he meet you. Join with him, and 'tis well.

{Enter La Foole.}

See, here comes your antagonist, but take you no notice, but be very jovial.

LA FOOLE.

Are the ladies come, Sir John Daw, and your mistress?

{Exit Daw.}

Sir Dauphine! You are exceeding welcome, and honest Master Clerimont. Where's my cousin? Did you see no collegiates, gentlemen?

DAUPHINE.

Collegiates! Do you not hear, Sir Amorous, how you are abused?

LA FOOLE.

How, sir!

CLERIMONT.

Will you speak so kindly to Sir John Daw, that has done you such an affront?

LA FOOLE.

Wherein, gentlemen? Let me be a suitor to you to know, I beseech you!

CLERIMONT.

Why, sir, his mistress is married today to Sir Dauphine's uncle, your cousin's neighbour, and he has diverted all the ladies and all your company thither, to frustrate your provision and stick a disgrace upon you. He was here now to have en-

ticed us away from you too, but we told him his own, I think.

LA FOOLE.

Has Sir John Daw wronged me so inhumanly?

DAUPHINE.

He has done it, Sir Amorous, most maliciously, and treacherously; but if you'll be ruled by us, you shall quit him, i' faith.

LA FOOLE.

Good gentlemen, I'll make one, believe it! How, I pray?

DAUPHINE.

Marry, sir, get me your pheasants, and your godwits, and your best meat, and dish it in silver dishes of your cousin's presently, and say nothing, but clap me a clean towel about you, like a sewer, and bare-headed march afore it with a good confidence – 'tis but over the way, hard by – and we'll second you, where you shall set it o' the board, and bid 'em welcome to't, which shall show 'tis yours and disgrace his preparation utterly; and for your cousin, whereas she should be troubled here at home with care of making and giving welcome, she shall transfer all that labour thither and be a principal guest herself, sit ranked with the college-honours, and be honoured, and have her health drunk as often, as bare, and as loud as the best of 'em.

LA FOOLE.

I'll go tell her presently. It shall be done, that's resolved.

{Exit.}

CLERIMONT.

I thought he would not hear it out, but 'twould take him.

DAUPHINE.

Well, there be guests and meat now; how shall we do for music?

CLERIMONT.

The smell of the venison going through the street will invite one noise of fiddlers or other.

DAUPHINE.

I would it would call the trumpeters thither.

CLERIMONT.

Faith, there is hope; they have intelligence of all feasts. There's good correspondence betwixt them and the London cooks. 'Tis twenty to one but we have 'em.

DAUPHINE.

'Twill be a most solemn day for my uncle, and an excellent fit of mirth for us.

CLERIMONT.

Ay, if we can hold up the emulation betwixt Foole and Daw, and never bring them to expostulate.

DAUPHINE.

Tut, flatter 'em both, as Truewit says, and you may take their understandings in a purse-net. They'll believe themselves to be just such men as we make 'em, neither more nor less. They have nothing, not the use of their senses, but by tradition.

{La Foole} enters like a sewer.

CLERIMONT.

See! Sir Amorous has his towel on already. Have you persuaded your cousin?

LA FOOLE.

Yes, 'tis very feasible: she'll do anything, she says, rather than the La Fooles shall be disgraced.

DAUPHINE.

She is a noble kinswoman. It will be such a pestling device, Sir Amorous! It will pound all your enemy's practices to powder and blow him up with his own mine, his own train.

LA FOOLE.

Nay, we'll give fire, I warrant you.

CLERIMONT.

But you must carry it privately, without any noise, and take no notice by any means –

{Enter Otter.}

OTTER.

Gentlemen, my princess says you shall have all her silver dishes, *festinate;* and she's gone to alter her tire a little and go with you –

CLERIMONT.

And yourself too, Captain Otter.

DAUPHINE.

By any means, sir.

OTTER.

Yes, sir, I do mean it; but I would entreat my cousin Sir Amorous, and you gentlemen, to be suitors to my princess, that I may carry my bull and my bear, as well as my horse.

CLERIMONT.

That you shall do, Captain Otter.

LA FOOLE.

My cousin will never consent, gentlemen.

DAUPHINE.

She must consent, Sir Amorous, to reason.

LA FOOLE.

Why, she says they are no decorum among ladies.

OTTER.

But they are *decora*, and that's better, sir.

CLERIMONT.

Ay, she must hear argument. Did not Pasiphae, who was a queen, love a bull? And was not Callisto, the mother of Arcas, turned into a bear and made a star, Mistress Ursula, i' the heavens?

OTTER.

Oh God, that I could ha' said as much! I will have these stories painted i' the Bear Garden, *ex Ovidii Metamorphosi.*

DAUPHINE.

Where is your princess, captain? Pray 'be our leader.

OTTER.

That I shall, sir.

CLERIMONT.

Make haste, good Sir Amorous.

{Exeunt.}

ACT THREE

Scene Four

{Enter} Morose, Epicoene, Parson, Cutbeard.

MOROSE.

Sir, there's an angel for yourself, and a brace of angels for your cold. Muse not at this manage of my bounty. It is fit we should thank fortune double to nature, for any benefit she confers upon us; besides, it is your imperfection, but my solace.

PARSON.

I thank your worship, so is it mine now.

The Parson speaks as having a cold.

MOROSE.

What says he, Cutbeard?

CUTBEARD.

He says *praesto*, sir: whensoever your worship needs him, he can be ready with the like. He got this cold with sitting up late and singing catches with cloth-workers.

MOROSE.

No more. I thank him.

PARSON.

God keep your worship and give you much joy with your fair spouse. Umh, umh.

He coughs.

MOROSE.

Oh, oh! Stay, Cutbeard! Let him give me five shillings of my money back. As it is bounty to reward benefits, so is it equity to mulct injuries. I will have it. What says he?

CUTBEARD.

He cannot change it, sir.

MOROSE.

It must be changed.

CUTBEARD.

{*Aside to Parson*}. Cough again.

MOROSE.

What says he?

CUTBEARD.

He will cough out the rest, sir.

PARSON.

Umh, umh, umh.

{*Coughs*} *again.*

MOROSE.

Away, away with him, stop his mouth, away, I forgive it –

{*Exit Cutbeard with Parson.*}

EPICOENE.

Fie, Master Morose, that you will use this violence to a man of the church.

MOROSE.

How!

EPICOENE.

It does not become your gravity or breeding – as you pretend in court – to have offered this outrage on a waterman, or any more boist'rous creature, much less on a man of his civil coat.

MOROSE.

You can speak then!

EPICOENE.

Yes, sir.

MOROSE.

Speak out, I mean.

EPICOENE.

Ay, sir. Why, did you think you had married a statue? or a motion only? one of the French puppets with the eyes turned with a wire? or some innocent out of the hospital, that would stand with her hands thus, and a plaice-mouth, and look upon you?

MOROSE.

Oh immodesty! A manifest woman! What, Cutbeard!

EPICOENE.

Nay, never quarrel with Cutbeard, sir, it is too late now. I confess it doth bate somewhat of the modesty I had, when I writ simply maid; but I hope I shall make it a stock still competent to the estate and dignity of your wife.

MOROSE.

She can talk!

EPICOENE.

Yes, indeed, sir.

MOROSE.

What sirrah! None of my knaves there?

{*Enter Mute.*}

Where is this imposter, Cutbeard?

{*Mute makes signs.*}

EPICOENE.

Speak to him, fellow, speak to him. I'll have none of this coacted, unnatural dumbness in my house, in a family where I govern.

{*Exit Mute.*}

MOROSE.

She is my regent already! I have married a Penthesilea, a Semiramis, sold my liberty to a distaff!

ACT THREE

Scene Five

{*Enter*} *Truewit.*

TRUEWIT.

Where's Master Morose?

MOROSE.

Is he come again? Lord have mercy upon me!

TRUEWIT.

I wish you all joy, Mistress Epicoene, with your grave and honourable match.

EPICOENE.

I return you the thanks, Master Truewit, so friendly a wish deserves.

MOROSE.

She has acquaintance too!

TRUEWIT.

God save you, sir, and give you all contentment in your fair choice here. Before I was the bird of night to you, the owl, but now I am the messenger of peace, a dove, and bring you the glad wishes of many friends, to the celebration of this good hour.

MOROSE.

What hour, sir?

TRUEWIT.

Your marriage hour, sir. I commend your resolution, that, notwithstanding all the dangers I laid afore you, in the voice of a night-crow, would yet go on, and be yourself. It shows you are a man constant to your own ends, and upright to your purposes, that would not be put off with left-handed cries.

MOROSE.

How should you arrive at the knowledge of so much?

TRUEWIT.

Why, did you ever hope, sir, committing the secrecy of it to a barber, that less than the whole town should know it? You might as well ha' told it the conduit, or the bakehouse, or the infantry that follow the court, and with more security. Could your gravity forget so old and noted a remnant as *lippis et tonsoribus notum*? Well, sir, forgive it yourself now, the fault, and be communicable with your friends. Here will be three or four fashionable ladies from the college to visit you presently, and their train of minions and followers.

MOROSE.

Bar my doors! Bar my doors! Where are all my eaters, my mouths now?

{*Enter Servants.*}

Bar up my doors, you varlets!

EPICOENE.

He is a varlet that stirs to such an office. Let 'em stand open. I would see him that dares move his eyes toward it. Shall I have a barricado made against my friends, to be barred of any pleasure they can bring in to me with honourable visitation?

{*Exit Servants.*}

MOROSE.

Oh Amazonian impudence!

TRUEWIT.

Nay, faith, in this, sir, she speaks but reason, and methinks is more continent than you. Would you go to bed so presently, sir, afore noon? A man of your head and hair should owe more to that reverend ceremony, and not mount the marriage-bed like a town bull or a mountain goat, but stay the due season, and ascend it then with religion and fear. Those delights are to be steeped in the humour and silence of the night; and give the day to other open pleasures and jollities of feast, of music, of revels, of discourse: we'll have all, sir, that may make your hymen high and happy.

MOROSE.

Oh, my torment, my torment!

TRUEWIT.

Nay, if you endure the first half hour, sir, so tediously, and with this irksomeness, what comfort or hope can this fair gentlewoman make to herself hereafter, in the consideration of so many years as are to come –

MOROSE.

Of my affliction. Good sir, depart and let her do it alone.

TRUEWIT.

I have done, sir.

MOROSE.

That cursed barber!

TRUEWIT.

Yes, faith, a cursed wretch indeed, sir.

MOROSE.

I have married his cittern, that's common to all men. Some plague above the plague –

TRUEWIT.

All Egypt's ten plagues –

MOROSE.

Revenge me on him.

TRUEWIT.

'Tis very well, sir. If you laid on a curse or two more, I'll assure you he'll bear 'em. As, that he may get the pox with seeking to cure it, sir? Or, that while he is curling another man's hair, his own may drop off? Or, for burning some male bawd's lock, he may have his brain beat out with the curling-iron?

MOROSE.

No, let the wretch live wretched. May he get the itch, and his shop so lousy as no man dare come at him, nor he come at no man.

TRUEWIT.

Ay, and if he would swallow all his balls for pills, let not them purge him.

MOROSE.

Let his warming-pan be ever cold.

TRUEWIT.

A perpetual frost underneath it, sir.

MOROSE.

Let him never hope to see fire again.

TRUEWIT.

But in hell, sir.

MOROSE.

His chairs be always empty, his scissors rust, and his combs mould in their cases.

TRUEWIT.

Very dreadful that! And may he lose the invention, sir, of carving lanterns in paper.

MOROSE.

Let there be no bawd carted that year to employ a basin of his, but let him be glad to eat his sponge for bread.

TRUEWIT.

And drink lotium to it, and much good do him.

MOROSE.

Or, for want of bread –

TRUEWIT.

Eat ear-wax, sir. I'll help you. Or, draw his own teeth and add them to the lute-string.

MOROSE.

No, beat the old ones to powder and make bread of them.

TRUEWIT.

Yes, make meal o' the millstones.

MOROSE.

May all the botches and burns that he has cured on others break out upon him.

TRUEWIT.

And he now forget the cure of 'em in himself, sir; or, if he do remember it, let him ha' scraped all his linen into lint for't, and have not a rag left him to set up with.

MOROSE.

Let him never set up again, but have the gout in his hands forever. Now no more, sir.

TRUEWIT.

Oh, that last was too high set! You might go less with him, i' faith, and be revenged enough; as, that he be never able to new-paint his pole –

MOROSE.

Good sir, no more. I forgot myself.

TRUEWIT.

Or, want credit to take up with a comb-maker –

MOROSE.

No more, sir.

TRUEWIT.

Or, having broken his glass in a former despair, fall now into a much greater, of ever getting another –

MOROSE.

I beseech you, no more.

TRUEWIT.

Or, that he never be trusted with trimming of any but chimney-sweepers –

MOROSE.

Sir –

TRUEWIT.

Or, may he cut a collier's throat with his razor by chance-medley, and yet hang for't.

MOROSE.

I will forgive him, rather than hear any more. I beseech you, sir.

ACT THREE

Scene Six

{*Enter*} *Daw, Haughty, Centaure, Mavis, Trusty.*

DAW.

This way, madam.

MOROSE.

Oh, the sea breaks in upon me! Another flood! An inundation! I shall be o'erwhelmed with noise. It beats already at my shores. I feel an earthquake in myself for't.

DAW.

{*Kissing Epicoene*}. 'Give you joy, mistress.

MOROSE.

Has she servants too!

DAW.

I have brought some ladies here to see and know you.

She kisses them severally as he presents them.

My Lady Haughty, this my Lady Centaure, Mistress Dol Mavis, Mistress Trusty, my Lady Haughty's woman. Where's your husband? Let's see him: can he endure no noise? Let me come to him.

MOROSE.

What nomenclator is this!

TRUEWIT.

Sir John Daw, sir, your wife's servant, this.

MOROSE.

A Daw, and her servant! Oh, 'tis decreed, 'tis decreed of me, and she have such servants.

{*Makes to go out.*}

TRUEWIT.

Nay, sir, you must kiss the ladies, you must not go away now; they come toward you to seek you out.

HAUGHTY.

I' faith, Master Morose, would you steal a marriage thus, in the midst of so many friends, and not acquaint us? Well, I'll kiss you, notwithstanding the justice of my quarrel. You shall give me leave, mistress, to use a becoming familiarity with your husband.

EPICOENE.

Your ladyship does me an honour in it, to let me know he is so worthy your favour; as you have done both him and me grace to visit so unprepared a pair to entertain you.

MOROSE.

Compliment! Compliment!

EPICOENE.

But I must lay the burden of that upon my servant here.

HAUGHTY.

It shall not need, Mistress Morose; we will all bear, rather than one shall be oppressed.

MOROSE.

I know it, and you will teach her the faculty, if she be to learn it.

{*The collegiates talk apart with Truewit.*}

HAUGHTY.

Is this the silent women?

CENTAURE

Nay, she has found her tongue since she was married, Master Truewit says.

HAUGHTY.

Oh, Master Truewit! 'Save you. What kind of creature is your bride here? She speaks, methinks!

TRUEWIT.

Yes, madam, believe it, she is a gentlewoman of very absolute behaviour and of a good race.

HAUGHTY.

And Jack Daw told us she could not speak.

TRUEWIT.

So it was carried in plot, madam, to put her upon this old fellow, by Sir Dauphine, his nephew, and one or two more of us; but she is a woman of an excellent assurance, and an extraordinary happy wit and tongue. You shall see her make rare sport with Daw ere night.

HAUGHTY.

And he brought us to laugh at her!

TRUEWIT

That falls out often, madam, that he that thinks himself the master-wit is the master-fool. I assure your ladyship, ye cannot laugh at her.

HAUGHTY.

No, we'll have her to the college: and she have wit, she shall be one of us! Shall she not, Centaure? We'll make her a collegiate.

CENTAURE.

Yes, faith, madam, and Mavis and she will set up a side.

TRUEWIT.

Believe it, madam, and Mistress Mavis, she will sustain her part.

MAVIS.

I'll tell you that when I have talked with her and tried her.

HAUGHTY.

Use her very civilly, Mavis.

MAVIS.

So I will, madam.

{*Mavis walks apart with Epicoene.*}

MOROSE.

Blessed minute, that they would whisper thus ever.

TRUEWIT.

In the meantime, madam, would but your ladyship help to vex him a little: you know his disease, talk to him about the wedding-ceremonies, or call for your gloves, or –

HAUGHTY.

Let me alone. Centaure, help me. Master bridegroom, where are you?

MOROSE.

Oh, it was too miraculously good to last!

HAUGHTY.

We see no ensigns of a wedding here, no character of a bridal: where be our scarfs and our gloves? I pray you give 'em us. Let's know your bride's colours and yours at least.

CENTAURE.

Alas, madam, he has provided none.

MOROSE.

Had I known your ladyship's painter, I would.

HAUGHTY.

He has given it you, Centaure i' faith. But do you hear, Master Morose, a jest will not absolve you in this manner. You that have sucked the milk of the court, and from thence have been brought up to the very strong meats and wine of it, been a courtier from the biggin to the night-cap, as we may say, and you to offend in such a high point of ceremony as this, and let your nuptials want all marks of solemnity! How much plate have you lost today – if you had but regarded your profit – what gifts, what friends, through your mere rusticity?

MOROSE.

Madam –

HAUGHTY.

Pardon me, sir, I must insinuate your errors to you. No gloves? No garters? No scarfs? No epithalamium? No masque?

DAW.

Yes, madam, I'll make an epithalamium, I promised my mistress, I have begun it already: will your ladyship hear it?

HAUGHTY.

Ay, good Jack Daw.

MOROSE.

Will it please your ladyship command a chamber and be private with your friend? You shall have your choice of rooms to retire to after; my whole house is yours. I know it hath been your ladyship's errand into the city at other times, however now you have been unhappily diverted upon me; but I shall be loath to break any honourable custom of your ladyship's. And therefore, good madam –

EPICOENE.

Come, you are a rude bridgroom, to entertain ladies of honour in this fashion.

CENTAURE.

He is a rude groom indeed.

TRUEWIT.

By that light, you deserve to be grafted, and have your horns reach from one side of the island to the other. – {*Aside to Morose.*} Do not mistake me, sir; I but speak this to give the ladies some heart again, not for any malice to you.

MOROSE.

Is this your bravo, ladies?

TRUEWIT.

As God help me, if you utter such another word, I'll take mistress bride in and begin to you in a very sad cup, do you see? Go to, know your friends and such as love you.

ACT THREE

Scene Seven

{*Enter*} *Clerimont* {*with Musicians*}.

CLERIMONT.
By your leave, ladies. Do you want any music? I have brought you variety of noises. Play, sirs, all of you.

Music of all sorts.

MOROSE.
Oh, a plot, a plot, a plot, a plot upon me! This day I shall be their anvil to work on, they will grate me asunder. 'Tis worse than the noise of a saw.

CLERIMONT.
No, they are hair, rosin, and guts. I can give you the receipt.

TRUEWIT.
Peace, boys.

CLERIMONT.
Play, I say.

TRUEWIT.
Peace, rascals. — You see who's your friend now, sir? Take courage, put on a martyr's resolution. Mock down all their attemptings with patience. 'Tis but a day, and I would suffer heroically. Should an ass exceed me in fortitude? No. You betray your infirmity with your hanging dull ears, and make them insult: bear up bravely and constantly.

La Foole {with Servants} passes over sewing the meat, {followed by Mistress Otter}.

Look you here, sir, what honour is done you unexpected by your nephew: a wedding-dinner come, and a knight-sewer before it, for the more reputation; and fine Mistress Otter, your neighbour, in the rump or tail of it.

MOROSE.
Is that Gorgon, that Medusa come? Hide me, hide me!

TRUEWIT.
I warrant you, sir, she will not transform you. Look upon her with a good courage. Pray you entertain her and conduct your guests in. No? — Mistress bride, will you entreat in the ladies? Your bridegroom is so shamefaced here –

EPICOENE.
Will it please your ladyship, madam?

HAUGHTY.
With the benefit of your company, mistress.

EPICOENE.
Servant, pray you perform your duties.

DAW.
And glad to be commanded, mistress.

CENTAURE.
How like you her wit, Mavis?

MAVIS.
Very prettily absolutely well.

MISTRESS OTTER.
{*Trying to take precedence*}. 'Tis my place.

MAVIS.
You shall pardon me, Mistress Otter.

MISTRESS OTTER.
Why, I am a collegiate.

MAVIS.
But not in ordinary.

MISTRESS OTTER.
But I am.

MAVIS.
We'll dispute that within.

{*Exit Daw with ladies.*}

CLERIMONT.
Would this had lasted a little longer.

TRUEWIT.
And that they had sent for the heralds.

{*Enter Otter.*}

Captain Otter, what news?

OTTER.
I have brought my bull, bear, and horse in private, and yonder are the trumpeters without, and the drum, gentlemen.

The drum and trumpets sound.

MOROSE.
Oh, oh, oh!

OTTER.

And we will have a rouse in each of 'em anon, for bold Britons, i' faith.

{*They sound again.*}

MOROSE.

Oh, oh, oh!

{*Exit Morose.*}

ALL.

Follow, follow, follow!

{*Exeunt.*}

ACT FOUR

Scene One

{*Enter*} *Truewit, Clerimont.*

TRUEWIT.

Was there ever poor bridegroom so tormented? or man, indeed?

CLERIMONT.

I have not read of the like in the chronicles of the land.

TRUEWIT.

Sure, he cannot but go to a place of rest after all this purgatory.

CLERIMONT.

He may presume it, I think.

TRUEWIT.

The spitting, the coughing, the laughter, the neezing, the farting, dancing, noise of the music, and her masculine and loud commanding and urging the whole family, makes him think he has married a Fury.

CLERIMONT.

And she carries it up bravely.

TRUEWIT.

Ay, she takes any occasion to speak: that's the height on't.

CLERIMONT.

And how soberly Dauphine labours to satsify him that it was none of his plot!

TRUEWIT.

And has almost brought him to the faith i' the article.

{*Enter Dauphine.*}

Here he comes. – Where is he now? What's become of him, Dauphine?

DAUPHINE.

Oh, hold me up a little, I shall go away i' the jest else. He has got on his whole nest of night-caps, and locked himself up i' the top o' the house, as high as ever he can climb from the noise. I peeped in at a cranny and saw him sitting over a cross-beam o' the roof, like him o' the saddler's horse in Fleet Street, upright; and he will sleep there.

CLERIMONT.

But where are your collegiates?

DAUPHINE.

Withdrawn with the bride in private.

TRUEWIT.

Oh, they are instructing her i' the college grammar. If she have grace with them, she knows all their secrets instantly.

CLERIMONT.

Methinks the Lady Haughty looks well today, for all my dispraise of her i' the morning. I think I shall come about to thee again, Truewit.

TRUEWIT.

Believe it, I told you right. Women ought to repair the losses time and years have made i' their features with dressings. And an intelligent woman, if she know by herself the least defect, will be most curious to hide it; and it becomes her. If she be short, let her sit much, lest when she stands she be thought to sit. If she have an ill foot, let her wear her gown the longer and her shoe the thinner. If a fat hand and scald nails, let her carve the less, and act in gloves. If a sour breath, let her never discourse fasting, and always talk at her distance. If she have black and rugged teeth, let her offer the less at laughter, especially if she laugh wide and open.

CLERIMONT.

Oh, you shall have some women, when they laugh, you would think they brayed, it is so rude, and –

TRUEWIT.

Ay, and others that will stalk i' their gait like an ostrich, and take huge strides. I cannot endure such a sight. I love measure i' the feet and number i' the voice: they are gentlenesses that oft-times draw no less than the face.

DAUPHINE.

How cam'st thou to study these creatures so exactly? I would thou wouldst make me a proficient.

TRUEWIT.

Yes, but you must leave to live i' your chamber, then, a month together upon *Amadis de Gaule* or *Don Quixote*, as you are wont, and come abroad where the matter is frequent, to court, to tiltings, public shows and feasts, to plays, and church sometimes: thither they come to show their new tires too, to see and to be seen. In these places a man shall find whom to love, whom to play with, whom to touch once, whom to hold ever. The variety arrests his judgement. A wench to please a man comes not down dropping from the ceiling, as he lies on his back droning a tobacco-pipe. He must go where she is.

DAUPHINE.

Yes, and be never the near.

TRUEWIT.

Out, heretic! That diffidence makes thee worthy it should be so.

CLERIMONT.

He says true to you, Dauphine.

DAUPHINE.

Why?

TRUEWIT.

A man should not doubt to overcome any woman. Think he can vanquish 'em, and he shall; for though they deny, their desire is to be tempted. Penelope herself cannot hold out long. Ostend, you saw, was taken at last. You must perséver and hold to your purpose. They would solicit us, but that they are afraid. Howsoever, they wish in their hearts we should solicit them. Praise 'em, flatter 'em, you shall never want eloquence or trust; even the chastest delight to feel themselves that way rubbed. With praises you must mix kisses too. If they take them, they'll take more. Though they strive, they would be overcome.

CLERIMONT.

Oh, but a man must beware of force.

TRUEWIT.

It is to them an acceptable violence, and has oft-times the place of the greatest courtesy. She that might have been forced, and you let her go free without touching, though she then seem to thank you, will ever hate you after; and glad i' the face, is assuredly sad at the heart.

CLERIMONT.

But all women are not to be taken all ways.

TRUEWIT.

'Tis true. No more than all birds or all fishes. If you appear learned to an ignorant wench, or jocund to a sad, or witty to a foolish, why, she presently begins to mistrust herself. You must approach them i' their own height, their own line; for the contrary makes many that fear to commit themselves to noble and worthy fellows run into the embraces of a rascal. If she love wit, give verses, though you borrow 'em of a friend, or buy 'em, to have good. If valour, talk of your sword, and be frequent in the mention of quarrels, though you be staunch in fighting. If activity, be seen o' your barbary often, or leaping over stools, for the credit of your back. If she love good clothes or dressing, have your learned council about you every morning, your French tailor, barber, linener, *et cetera*. Let your powder, your glass, and your comb be your dearest acquaintance. Take more care for the ornament of your head than the safety, and wish the commonwealth rather troubled than a hair about you. That will take her. Then if she be covetous and craving, do you promise anything, and perform sparingly; so shall you keep her in appetite still. Seem as you would give, but be like a barren field that yields little, or unlucky dice to foolish and hoping gamesters. Let your gifts be slight and dainty, rather than precious. Let cunning be above cost. Give cherries at time of year, or apricots; and say they were sent you out o' the country, though you bought 'em in Cheapside. Admire her tires, like her in all fashions, compare her in every habit to some deity, invent excellent dreams to flatter her, and riddles; or, if she be a great one, perform always the second parts to her: like what she likes, praise whom she praises, and fail not to make the household and servants yours, yea, the whole family, and salute 'em by their names – 'tis but light cost if you can purchase 'em so – and make her physician your pensioner, and her chief woman. Nor will it be out of your gain to make love to her too, so she follow, not usher, her lady's pleasure. All blabbing is taken away when she comes to be a part of the crime.

DAUPHINE.
On what courtly lap hast thou late slept, to come forth so sudden and absolute a courtling?

TRUEWIT.
Good faith, I should rather question you, that are so heark'ning after these mysteries. I begin to suspect your diligence, Dauphine. Speak, art thou in love in earnest?

DAUPHINE.
Yes, by my troth, am I; 'twere ill dissembling before thee.

TRUEWIT.
With which of 'em, I pray thee?

DAUPHINE.
With all the collegiates.

CLERIMONT.
Out on thee! We'll keep you at home, believe it, i' the stable, and you be such a stallion.

TRUEWIT.
No; I like him well. Men should love wisely, and all women: some one for the face, and let her please the eye; another for the skin, and let her please the touch; and third for the voice, and let her please the ear; and where the objects mix, let the senses so too. Thou wouldst think it strange if I should make 'em all in love with thee afore night!

DAUPHINE.
I would say thou hadst the best philtre i' the world, and couldst do more than Madam Medea or Doctor Forman.

TRUEWIT.
If I do not, let me play the mountebank for my meat while I live, and the bawd for my drink.

DAUPHINE.
So be it, I say.

ACT FOUR

Scene Two

{Enter} Otter {carrying his cups}, Daw, La Foole.

OTTER.
Oh lord, gentlemen, how my knights and I have missed you here!

CLERIMONT.
Why, captain, what service, what service?

OTTER.
To see me bring up my bull, bear, and horse to fight.

DAW.
Yes, faith, the captain says we shall be his dogs to bait 'em.

DAUPHINE.
A good employment.

TRUEWIT.
Come on, let's see a course then.

LA FOOLE.
I am afraid my cousin will be offended if she come.

OTTER.
Be afraid of nothing. Gentlemen, I have placed the drum and the trumpets and one to give 'em the sign when you are ready. Here's my bull for myself, and my bear for Sir John Daw, and my horse for Sir Amorous. Now, set your foot to mine, and yours to his, and –

LA FOOLE.
Pray God my cousin come not.

OTTER.
Saint George and Saint Andrew, fear no cousins. Come,

sound, sound! *Et rauco strepuerunt cornua cantu.*

{*Drum and trumpets sound. They drink.*}

TRUEWIT.
Well said, captain, i' faith; well fought at the bull.

CLERIMONT.
Well held at the bear.

TRUEWIT.
'Loo, 'loo, captain!

DAUPHINE.
Oh, the horse has kicked off his dog already.

LA FOOLE.
I cannot drink it, as I am a knight.

TRUEWIT.
Gods so! Off with his spurs, somebody.

LA FOOLE.
It goes again my conscience. My cousin will be angry with it.

DAW.
I ha' done mine.

TRUEWIT.
You fought high and fair, Sir John.

CLERIMONT.
At the head.

DAUPHINE.
Like an excellent bear-dog.

CLERIMONT.
{*Aside to Daw*}. You take no notice of the business, I hope.

DAW.
{*Aside to Clerimont*}. Not a word, sir; you see we are jovial.

OTTER.
Sir Amorous, you must not equivocate. It must be pulled down, for all my cousin.

CLERIMONT.
{*Aside to La Foole*}. 'Sfoot, if you take not your drink, they'll think you are discontented with something; you'll betray all if you take the least notice.

LA FOOLE.
{*Aside to Clerimont*}. Not I, I'll both drink and talk then.

OTTER.
You must pull the horse on his knees, Sir Amorous. Fear no cousins: *jacta est alea.*

TRUEWIT.
{*Aside to Dauphine and Clerimont*}. Oh, now he's in his vein, and bold. The least hint given him of his wife now will make him rail desperately.

CLERIMONT.
Speak to him of her.

TRUEWIT.
Do you, and I'll fetch her to the hearing of it.

{*Exit.*}

DAUPHINE.
Captain he-Otter, your she-Otter is coming, your wife.

OTTER.
Wife! Buz! *Titivilitium.* There's no such thing in nature. I confess, gentlemen, I have a cook, a laundress, a house-drudge, that serves my necessary turns and goes under that title; but he's an ass that will be so uxorious to tie his affections to one circle. Come, the name dulls appetite. Here, replenish again: another bout. Wives are nasty, sluttish animals.

{*Fills the cups.*}

DAUPHINE.
Oh captain!

OTTER.
As ever the earth bare, *tribus verbis.* Where's Master Truewit?

DAW.
He's slipped aside, sir.

CLERIMONT.
But you must drink and be jovial.

DAW.
Yes, give it me.

LA FOOLE.
And me too.

DAW.
Let's be jovial.

LA FOOLE.
As jovial as you will.

OTTER.

Agreed. Now you shall ha' the bear, cousin, and Sir John Daw the horse, and I'll ha' the bull still. Sound, Tritons o' the Thames. *Nunc est bibendum, nunc pede libero –*

{They drink.}

Morose speaks from above, the trumpets sounding.

MOROSE.

Villains, murderers, sons of the earth, and traitors, what do you there?

CLERIMONT.

Oh, now the trumpets have waked him we shall have his company.

OTTER.

A wife is a scurvy clogdogdo, an unlucky thing, a very foresaid bear-whelp, without any good fashion or breeding: *mala bestia.*

His wife is brought out to hear him {by Truewit}.

DAUPHINE.

Why did you marry one then, captain?

OTTER.

A pox – I married with six thousand pound, I. I was in love with that. I ha' not kissed my Fury these forty weeks.

CLERIMONT.

The more to blame you, captain.

TRUEWIT.

Nay, Mistress Otter, hear him a little first.

OTTER.

She has a breath worse than my grandmother's, *profecto.*

MISTRESS OTTER.

Oh treacherous liar! Kiss me, sweet Master Truewit, and prove him a slandering knave.

TRUEWIT.

I'll rather believe you, lady.

OTTER.

And she has a peruke that's like a pound of hemp made up in shoe-threads.

MISTRESS OTTER.

Oh viper, mandrake!

OTTER.

A most vile face! And yet she spends me forty pounds a year

in mercury and hogs' bones. All her teeth were made i' the Blackfriars, both her eyebrows i' the Strand, and her hair in Silver Street. Every part o' the town owns a piece of her.

MISTRESS OTTER.

I cannot hold.

OTTER.

She takes herself asunder still when she goes to bed, into some twenty boxes, and about next day noon is put together again, like a great German clock; and so comes forth and rings a tedious larum to the whole house, and then is quiet again for an hour, but for her quarters. – Ha' you done me right, gentlemen?

MISTRESS OTTER.

No, sir, I'll do you right with my quarters, with my quarters.

She falls upon him and beats him.

OTTER.

Oh hold, good princess!

TRUEWIT.

Sound, sound.

{Drum and trumpets sound.}

CLERIMONT.

A battle, a battle.

MISTRESS OTTER.

You notorious stinkardly bearward, does my breath smell?

OTTER.

Under correction, dear princess. Look to my bear and my horse, gentlemen.

MISTRESS OTTER.

Do I want teeth and eyebrows, thou bull-dog?

TRUEWIT.

Sound, sound still.

{They sound again.}

OTTER.

No, I protest, under correction –

MISTRESS OTTER.

Ay, now you are under correction, you protest; but you did not protest before correction, sir. Thou Judas, to offer to betray thy princess! I'll make thee an example –

Morose descends with a long sword.

MOROSE.
I will have no such examples in my house, Lady Otter.

MISTRESS OTTER.
Ah!

{*She runs off, followed by Daw, and La Foole.*}

MOROSE.
Mistress Mary Ambree, your examples are dangerous. – Rogues, hell-hounds, Stentors, out of my doors, you sons of noise and tumult, begot on an ill May-day, or when the galley-foist is afloat to Westminster! {*Drives out the Musicians.*} A trumpeter could not be conceived but then!

DAUPHINE.
What ails you, sir?

MOROSE.
They have rent my roof, walls and all my windows asunder, with their brazen throats.

{*Exit.*}

TRUEWIT.
Best follow him, Dauphine.

DAUPHINE.
So I will.

{*Exit.*}

CLERIMONT.
Where's Daw and La Foole?

OTTER.
They are both run away, sir. Good gentlemen, help to pacify my princess, and speak to the great ladies for me. Now must I go lie with the bears this fortnight, and keep out o' the way till my peace be made, for this scandal she has taken. Did you not see my bull-head, gentlemen?

CLERIMONT.
Is't not on, captain?

TRUEWIT.
No: – {*Aside to Clerimont.*} but he may make a new one, by that is on.

OTTER.
Oh, here 'tis. And you come over, gentlemen, and ask for Tom Otter, we'll go down to Ratcliffe, and have a course i' faith, for all these disasters. There's *bona spes* left.

TRUEWIT.
Away, captain, get off while you are well.

{*Exit Otter.*}

CLERIMONT.
I am glad we are rid of him.

TRUEWIT.
You had never been, unless we had put his wife upon him. His humour is as tedious at last, as it was ridiculous at first.

ACT FOUR

Scene Three

{*Enter*} Haughty, Mistress Otter, Mavis, Daw, La Foole, Centaure, Epicoene. {*Truewit and Clerimont move aside and observe.*}

HAUGHTY.
We wondered why you shrieked so, Mistress Otter.

MISTRESS OTTER.
Oh God, madam, he came down with a huge long naked weapon in both his hands, and looked so dreadfully! Sure, he's beside himself.

MAVIS.
Why, what made you there, Mistress Otter?

MISTRESS OTTER.
Alas, Mistress Mavis, I was chastising my subject, and thought nothing of him.

DAW.
{*To Epicoene*}. Faith, mistress, you must do so too. Learn to chastise. Mistress Otter corrects her husband, so, he dares not speak but under correction.

LA FOOLE.
And with his hat off to her: 'twould do you good to see.

HAUGHTY.
In sadness, 'tis good and mature counsel: practise it, Morose. I'll call you Morose still now, as I call Centaure and Mavis: we four will be all one.

CENTAURE.
And you'll come to the college and live with us?

HAUGHTY.
Make him give milk and honey.

MAVIS.

Look how you manage him at first, you shall have him ever after.

CENTAURE.

Let him allow you your coach and four horses, your woman, your chambermaid, your page, your gentleman-usher, your French cook, and four grooms.

HAUGHTY.

And go with us to Bedlam, to the china-houses, and to the Exchange.

CENTAURE.

It will open the gate to your fame.

HAUGHTY.

Here's Centaure has immortalized herself with taming of her wild male.

MAVIS.

Ay, she has done the miracle of the kingdom.

EPICOENE.

But ladies, do you count it lawful to have such plurality of servants, and do 'em all graces?

HAUGHTY.

Why not? Why should women deny their favours to men? Are they the poorer, or the worse?

DAW.

Is the Thames the less for the dyer's water, mistress?

LA FOOLE.

Or a torch for lighting many torches?

TRUEWIT.

{Aside}. Well said, La Foole; what a new one he has got!

CENTAURE.

They are empty losses women fear in this kind.

HAUGHTY.

Besides, ladies should be mindful of the approach of age, and let no time want his due use. The best of our days pass first.

MAVIS.

We are rivers that cannot be called back, madam: she that now excludes her lovers may live to lie a forsaken beldame in a frozen bed.

CENTAURE.

'Tis true, Mavis; and who will wait on us to coach then? or write, or tell us the news then? make anagrams of our names,

and invite us to the cockpit, and kiss our hands all the play-time, and draw their weapons for our honours?

HAUGHTY.

Not one.

DAW.

Nay, my mistress is not altogether unintelligent of these things; here be in presence have tasted of her favours.

CLERIMONT.

{Aside}. What a neighing hobby-horse is this!

EPICOENE.

But not with intent to boast 'em again, servant. And have you those excellent receipts, madam, to keep yourselves from bearing of children?

HAUGHTY.

Oh yes, Morose. How should we maintain our youth and beauty else? Many births of a woman make her old, as many crops make the earth barren.

ACT FOUR

Scene Four

{Enter} Morose, Dauphine; {they speak apart}.

MOROSE.

Oh my cursed angel, that instructed me to this fate!

DAUPHINE.

Why, sir?

MOROSE.

That I should be seduced by so foolish a devil as a barber will make!

DAUPHINE.

I would I had been worthy, sir, to have partaken your counsel; you should never have trusted it to such a minister.

MOROSE.

Would I could redeem it with the loss of an eye, nephew, a hand, or any other member.

DAUPHINE.

Marry, God forbid, sir, that you should geld yourself to anger your wife.

MOROSE.

So it would rid me of her! And that I did supererogatory penance, in a belfry, at Westminster Hall, i' the cockpit, at the fall of a stag, the Tower Wharf – what place is there else? – London Bridge, Paris Garden, Belinsgate, when the noises are at their height and loudest. Nay, I would sit out a play that were nothing but fights at sea, drum, trumpet, and target!

DAUPHINE.

I hope there shall be no such need, sir. Take patience, good uncle. This is but a day, and 'tis well worn too now.

MOROSE.

Oh, 'twill be so forever, nephew, I foresee it, forever. Strife and tumult are the dowry that comes with a wife.

TRUEWIT.

I told you so, sir, and you would not believe me.

MOROSE.

Alas, do not rub those wounds, Master Truewit, to blood again; 'twas my negligence. Add not affliction to affliction. I have perceived the effect of it, too late, in Madam Otter.

EPICOENE.

{*Coming forward*}. How do you, sir?

MOROSE.

Did you ever hear a more unnecessary question? As if she did not see! Why, I do as you see, empress, empress.

EPICOENE.

You are not well, sir! You look very ill! Something has distempered you.

MOROSE.

Oh horrible, monstrous impertinencies! Would not one of these have served? Do you think, sir? Would not one of these have served?

TRUEWIT.

Yes, sir, but these are but notes of female kindness, sir; certain tokens that she has a voice, sir.

MOROSE.

Oh, is't so? Come, and't be no otherwise – what say you?

EPICOENE.

How do you feel yourself, sir?

MOROSE.

Again that!

TRUEWIT.

Nay, look you, sir: you would be friends with your wife upon unconscionable terms, her silence –

EPICOENE.

They say you are run mad, sir.

MOROSE.

Not for love, I assure you, of you; do you see?

EPICOENE.

Oh lord, gentlemen! Lay hold on him for God's sake. What shall I do? Who's his physician – can you tell – that knows the state of his body best, that I might send for him? Good sir, speak. I'll send for one of my doctors else.

MOROSE.

What, to poison me, that I might die intestate and leave you possessed of all?

EPICOENE.

Lord, how idly he talks, and how his eyes sparkle! He looks green about the temples! Do you see what blue spots he has?

CLERIMONT.

Ay, it's melancholy.

EPICOENE.

Gentlemen, for heaven's sake counsel me. Ladies! Servant, you have read Pliny and Paracelsus: ne'er a word now to comfort a poor gentlewoman? Ay me! What fortune had I to marry a distracted man?

DAW.

I'll tell you, mistress –

TRUEWIT.

{*Aside*}. How rarely she holds it up!

{*Truewit and Clerimont prevent Morose from leaving.*}

MOROSE.

What mean you, gentlemen?

EPICOENE.

What will you tell me, servant?

DAW.

The disease in Greek is called μανια, in Latin *insania, furor, vel ecstasis melancholica*, that is, *egressio*, when a man *ex melancholico evadit fanaticus*.

MOROSE.

Shall I have a lecture read upon me alive?

DAW.

But he may be but *phreneticus* yet, mistress, and *phrenetis* is only *delirium* or so –

EPICOENE.

Ay, that is for the disease, servant; but what is this to the cure? We are sure enough of the disease.

MOROSE.

Let me go!

TRUEWIT.

Why, we'll entreat her to hold her peace, sir.

MOROSE.

Oh no, labour not to stop her. She is like a conduit-pipe that will gush out with more force when she opens again.

HAUGHTY.

I'll tell you, Morose, you must talk divinity to him altogether, or moral philosophy.

LA FOOLE.

Ay, and there's an excellent book of moral philosophy, madam, of Reynard the Fox and all the beasts, called *Doni's Philosophy*.

CENTAURE.

There is indeed, Sir Amorous La Foole.

MOROSE.

Oh misery!

LA FOOLE.

I have read it, my Lady Centaure, all over to my cousin here.

MISTRESS OTTER.

Ay, and 'tis a very good book as any is of the moderns.

DAW.

Tut, he must have Seneca read to him, and Plutarch and the ancients; the moderns are not for this disease.

CLERIMONT.

Why, you discommended them too today, Sir John.

DAW.

Ay, in some cases; but in these they are best, and Aristotle's *Ethics*.

MAVIS.

Say you so, Sir John? I think you are deceived: you took it upon trust.

HAUGHTY.

Where's Trusty, my woman? I'll end this difference. I prithee, Otter, call her. Her father and mother were both mad when they put her to me.

{*Exit Mistress Otter.*}

MOROSE.

I think so. – Nay, gentlemen, I am tame. This is but an exercise, I know, a marriage ceremony, which I must endure.

HAUGHTY.

And one of 'em – I know not which – was cured with *The Sick Man's Salve*, and the other with Greene's *Groat's-worth of Wit*.

TRUEWIT.

A very cheap cure, madam.

HAUGHTY.

Ay, it's very feasible.

{*Enter Mistress Otter with Trusty.*}

MISTRESS OTTER.

My lady called for you, Mistress Trusty; you must decide a controversy.

HAUGHTY.

Oh, Trusty, which was it you said, your father or your mother, that was cured with *The Sick Man's Salve*?

TRUSTY.

My mother, madam, with the *Salve*.

TRUEWIT.

Then it was *The Sick Woman's Salve*.

TRUSTY.

And my father with the *Groat's-worth of Wit*. But there was other means used: we had a preacher that would preach folk asleep still; and so they were prescribed to go to church by an old woman that was their physician, thrice a week –

EPICOENE.

To sleep?

TRUSTY.

Yes, forsooth; and every night they read themselves asleep on those books.

EPICOENE.

Good faith, it stands with great reason. I would I knew where to procure those books.

MOROSE.

Oh!

LA FOOLE.

I can help you with one of 'em, Mistress Morose, the *Groat's-worth of Wit*.

EPICOENE.

But I shall disfurnish you, Sir Amorous. Can you spare it?

LA FOOLE.

Oh, yes, for a week or so; I'll read it myself to him.

EPICOENE.

No, I must do that, sir; that must be my office.

MOROSE.

Oh, oh!

EPICOENE.

Sure, he would do well enough, if he could sleep.

MOROSE.

No, I should do well enough if you could sleep. Have I no friend that will make her drunk? or give her a little ladanum, or opium?

TRUEWIT.

Why, sir, she talks ten times worse in her sleep.

MOROSE.

How!

CLERIMONT.

Do you not know that, sir? Never ceases all night.

TRUEWIT.

And snores like a porcpisce.

MOROSE.

Oh, redeem me, fate, redeem me, fate! For how many causes may a man be divorced, nephew?

DAUPHINE.

I know not truly, sir.

TRUEWIT.

Some divine must resolve you in that, sir, or canon lawyer.

MOROSE.

I will not rest, I will not think of any other hope or comfort, till I know.

{*Exeunt Morose and Dauphine.*}

CLERIMONT.

Alas, poor man.

TRUEWIT.

You'll make him mad indeed, ladies, if you pursue this.

HAUGHTY.

No, we'll let him breathe now a quarter of an hour or so.

CLERIMONT.

By my faith, a large truce.

HAUGHTY.

Is that his keeper that is gone with him?

DAW.

It is his nephew, madam.

LA FOOLE.

Sir Dauphine Eugenie.

CENTAURE.

He looks like a very pitiful knight –

DAW.

As can be. This marriage has put him out of all.

LA FOOLE.

He has not a penny in his purse, madam –

DAW.

He is ready to cry all this day.

LA FOOLE.

A very shark, he set me i' the nick t'other night at primero.

TRUEWIT.

{*Aside*). How these swabbers talk!

CLERIMONT.

{*Aside*}. Ay, Otter's wine has swelled their humours above a spring-tide.

HAUGHTY.

Good Morose, let's go in again. I like your couches exceeding well: we'll go lie and talk there.

EPICOENE.

I wait on you, madam.

{*Exeunt Haughty, Centaure, Mavis, Trusty, La Foole and Daw.*}

TRUEWIT.

'Slight, I will have 'em as silent as signs, and their posts too, ere I ha' done. Do you hear, lady bride? I pray thee now, as thou art a noble wench, continue this discourse of Dauphine within; but praise him exceedingly. Magnify him with all the height of affection thou canst – I have some purpose in't – and but beat off these two rooks, Jack Daw and his fellow, with any discontentment hither, and I'll honour thee forever.

EPICOENE.

I was about it here. It angered me to the soul to hear 'em begin to talk so malapert.

TRUEWIT.

Pray thee perform it, and thou winn'st me an idolater to thee everlasting.

EPICOENE.

Will you go in and hear me do it?

TRUEWIT.

No, I'll stay here. Drive 'em out of your company, 'tis all I ask; which cannot be any way better done than by extolling Dauphine, whom they have so slighted.

EPICOENE.

I warrant you; you shall expect one of 'em presently.

{*Exit.*}

CLERIMONT.

What a cast of kastrils are these, to hawk after ladies thus?

TRUEWIT.

Ay, and strike at such an eagle as Dauphine.

CLERIMONT.

He will be mad when we tell him. Here he comes.

ACT FOUR

Scene Five

{*Enter*} *Dauphine.*

CLERIMONT.

Oh sir, you are welcome.

TRUEWIT.

Where's thine uncle?

DAUPHINE.

Run out o' doors in's night-caps to talk with a casuist about his divorce. It works admirably.

TRUEWIT.

Thou wouldst ha' said so and thou hadst been here! The ladies have laughed at thee most comically since thou went'st, Dauphine.

CLERIMONT.

And asked if thou wert thine uncle's keeper?

TRUEWIT.

And the brace of baboons answered yes, and said thou wert a pitiful poor fellow and didst live upon posts, and hadst nothing but three suits of apparel and some few benevolences that lords ga' thee to fool to 'em and swagger.

DAUPHINE.

Let me not live, I'll beat 'em. I'll bind 'em both to grand madam's bed-posts and have 'em baited with monkeys.

TRUEWIT.

Thou shalt not need, they shall be beaten to thy hand, Dauphine. I have an execution to serve upon 'em I warrant thee shall serve; trust my plot.

DAUPHINE.

Ay, you have many plots! So you had one to make all the wenches in love with me.

TRUEWIT.

Why, if I do not yet afore night, as near as 'tis, and that they do not every one invite thee and be ready to scratch for thee, take the mortgage of my wit.

CLERIMONT.

'Fore God, I'll be his witness; thou shalt have it, Dauphine; thou shalt be his fool forever if thou dost not.

TRUEWIT.

Agreed. Perhaps 'twill be the better estate. Do you observe this gallery, or rather lobby, indeed? Here are a couple of studies, at each end one: here will I act such a tragicomedy between the Guelphs and the Ghibellines, Daw and La Foole. Which of 'em comes out first will I seize on. You two shall be the chorus behind the arras, and whip out between the acts and speak. If I do not make 'em keep the peace for this remnant of the day, if not of the year, I have failed once – I hear Daw coming. Hide, and do not laugh, for God's sake.

{*Dauphine and Clerimont hide.*}
{*Enter Daw.*}

DAW.

Which is the way into the garden, trow?

TRUEWIT.

Oh, Jack Daw! I am glad I have met with you. In good faith, I must have this matter go no further between you. I must ha' it taken up.

DAW.

What matter, sir? Between whom?

TRUEWIT.

Come, you disguise it: Sir Amorous and you. If you love me, Jack, you shall make use of your philosophy now, for this once, and deliver me your sword. This is not the wedding the Centaurs were at, though there be a she-one here. The bride has entreated me I will see no blood shed at her bridal; you saw her whisper me erewhile.

{*Takes his sword.*}

DAW.

As I hope to finish Tacitus, I intend no murder.

TRUEWIT.

Do you not wait for Sir Amorous?

DAW.

Not I, by my knighthood.

TRUEWIT.

And your scholarship too?

DAW.

And my scholarship too.

TRUEWIT.

Go to, then I return you your sword, and ask you mercy; but put it not up, for you will be assaulted. I understood that you had apprehended it, and walked here to brave him, and that you had held your life contemptible in regard of your honour.

DAW.

No, no, no such thing, I assure you. He and I parted now as good friends as could be.

TRUEWIT.

Trust not you to that visor. I saw him since dinner with another face: I have known many men in my time vexed with losses, with deaths, and with abuses, but so offended a wight as Sir Amorous did I never see, or read of. For taking away his guests, sir, today, that's the cause, and he declares it behind your back with such threat'nings and contempts. He said to Dauphine you were the arrant'st ass –

DAW.

Ay, he may say his pleasure.

TRUEWIT.

And swears you are so protested a coward that he knows you will never do him any manly or single right, and therefore he will take his course.

DAW.

I'll give him any satisfaction, sir – but fighting.

TRUEWIT.

Ay, sir, but who knows what satisfaction he'll take? Blood he thirsts for, and blood he will have; and whereabouts on you he will have it, who knows but himself?

DAW.

I pray you, Master Truewit, be you a mediator.

TRUEWIT.

Well, sir, conceal yourself then in this study till I return.

He puts him up.

Nay, you must be content to be locked in; for, for mine own reputation, I would not have you seen to receive a public disgrace, while I have the matter in managing. Gods so, here he comes! Keep your breath close, that he do not hear you sigh. – In good faith, Sir Amorous, he is not this way; I pray you be merciful, do not murder him; he is a Christian as good as you; you are armed as if you sought a revenge on all his race. Good Dauphine, get him away from this place. I never knew a man's choler so high but he would speak to his friends, he would hear reason. – Jack Daw. Jack Daw! Asleep?

DAW.

Is he gone, Master Truewit?

TRUEWIT.

Ay, did you hear him?

DAW.

Oh God, yes.

TRUEWIT.

{*Aside*}. What a quick ear fear has!

DAW.

But is he so armed, as you say?

TRUEWIT.

Armed? Did you ever see a fellow set out to take possession?

DAW.

Ay, sir.

TRUEWIT.

That may give you some light to conceive of him; but 'tis nothing to the principal. Some false brother i' the house has furnished him strangely. Or, if it were out o' the house, it was Tom Otter.

DAW.

Indeed, he's a captain, and his wife is his kinswoman.

TRUEWIT.

He has got somebody's old two-hand sword, to mow you off at the knees. And that sword hath spawned such a dagger! – But then he is so hung with pikes, halberds, petronels, calivers, and muskets, that he looks like a justice of peace's hall; a man of two thousand a year is not sessed at so many weapons as he has on. There was never fencer challenged at so many several foils. You would think he meant to murder all Saint Pulchre's parish. If he could but victual himself for half a year in his breeches, he is sufficiently armed to overrun a country.

DAW.

Good lord, what means he, sir! I pray you, Master Truewit, be you a mediator.

TRUEWIT.

Well, I'll try if he will be appeased with a leg or an arm; if not, you must die once.

DAW.

I would be loath to lose my right arm, for writing madrigals.

TRUEWIT.

Why, if he will be satisfied with a thumb or a little finger, all's one to me. You must think I'll do my best.

DAW.

Good sir, do.

He puts him up again, and then {Dauphine and Clerimont} come forth.

CLERIMONT.

What has thou done?

TRUEWIT.

He will let me do nothing, man, he does all afore me; he offers his left arm.

CLERIMONT.

His left wing, for a Jack Daw.

DAUPHINE.

Take it by all means.

TRUEWIT.

How! Maim a man forever for a jest? What a conscience hast thou?

DAUPHINE.

'Tis no loss to him: he has no employment for his arms but to eat spoon-meat. Beside, as good maim his body as his reputation.

TRUEWIT.

He is a scholar and a Wit, and yet he does not think so. But he loses no reputation with us, for we all resolved him an ass before. To your places again.

CLERIMONT.

I pray thee let me be in at the other a little.

TRUEWIT.

Look, you'll spoil all: these be ever your tricks.

CLERIMONT.

No, but I could hit of some things that thou wilt miss, and thou wilt say are good ones.

TRUEWIT.

I warrant you. I pray forbear, I'll leave it off else.

DAUPHINE.

Come away, Clerimont.

{They hide.}

{Enter La Foole.}

TRUEWIT.

Sir Amorous!

LA FOOLE.

Master Truewit.

TRUEWIT.

Whither were you going?

LA FOOLE.

Down into the court to make water.

TRUEWIT.

By no means, sir; you shall rather tempt your breeches.

LA FOOLE.

Why, sir?

TRUEWIT.

{Opening the other door.} Enter here if you love your life.

LA FOOLE.

Why? Why?

TRUEWIT.
Question till your throat be cut, do; dally till the enraged soul find you.

LA FOOLE.
Who's that?

TRUEWIT.
Daw it is; will you in?

LA FOOLE.
Ay, ay, I'll in; what's the matter?

TRUEWIT.
Nay, if he had been cool enough to tell us that, there had been some hope to atone you, but he seems so implacably enraged.

LA FOOLE.
'Slight, let him rage. I'll hide myself.

TRUEWIT.
Do, good sir. But what have you done to him within that should provoke him thus? You have broke some jest upon him afore the ladies –

LA FOOLE.
Not I, never in my life broke jest upon any man. The bride was praising Sir Dauphine, and he went away in snuff, and I followed him, unless he took offence at me in his drink erewhile, that I would not pledge all the horse-full.

TRUEWIT.
By my faith, and that may be, you remember well; but he walks the round up and down, through every room o' the house, with a towel in his hand, crying, 'Where's La Foole? Who saw La Foole?' And when Dauphine and I demanded the cause, we can force no answer from him but 'Oh revenge, how sweet art thou! I will strangle him in this towel' – which leads us to conjecture that the main cause of his fury is for bringing your meat today, with a towel about you, to his discredit.

LA FOOLE.
Like enough. Why, and he be angry for that, I'll stay here till his anger be blown over.

TRUEWIT.
A good becoming resolution, sir. If you can put it on o' the sudden.

LA FOOLE.
Yes, I can put it on. Or I'll away into the country presently.

TRUEWIT.
How will you get out o' the house, sir? He knows you are i' the house, and he'll watch you this, se'en-night but he'll have you. He'll outwait a sergeant for you.

LA FOOLE.
Why then I'll stay here.

TRUEWIT.
You must think how to victual yourself in time then.

LA FOOLE.
Why, sweet Master Truewit, will you entreat my cousin Otter to send me a cold venison pasty, a bottle or two of wine, and a chamber-pot?

TRUEWIT.
A stool were better, sir, of Sir A-jax his invention.

LA FOOLE.
Ay, that will be better indeed; and a pallet to lie on.

TRUEWIT.
Oh, I would not advise you to sleep by any means.

LA FOOLE.
Would you not, sir? Why then I will not.

TRUEWIT.
Yet there's another fear –

LA FOOLE.
Is there, sir? What is't?

TRUEWIT.
No, he cannot break open this door with his foot, sure.

LA FOOLE.
I'll set my back against it, sir. I have a good back.

TRUEWIT.
But then if he should batter.

LA FOOLE.
Batter! If he dare, I'll have an action of batt'ry against him.

TRUEWIT.
Cast you the worst. He has sent for powder already, and what he will do with it, no man knows; perhaps blow up the corner o' the house where he suspects you are. Here he comes! In, quickly.

He feigns as if one were present, to fright the other, who is run in to hide himself.

I protest, Sir John Daw, he is not this way. What will you do?

Before God, you shall hang no petard here. I'll die rather. Will you not take my word? I never knew one but would be satisfied. – Sir Amorous, there's no standing out. He has made a petard of an old brass pot, to force your door. Think upon some satisfaction or terms to offer him.

LA FOOLE.

{Within}. Sir, I'll give him any satisfaction. I dare give any terms.

TRUEWIT.

You'll leave it to me then?

LA FOOLE.

Ay, sir. I'll stand to any conditions.

{Truewit} calls forth Clerimont and Dauphine.

TRUEWIT.

How now, what think you, sirs? Were't not a difficult thing to determine which of these two feared most?

CLERIMONT.

Yes, but this fears the bravest; the other a whiniling dastard, Jack Daw. But La Foole, a brave heroic coward! And is afraid in a great look and a stout accent. I like him rarely.

TRUEWIT.

Had it not been pity these two should ha' been concealed?

CLERIMONT.

Shall I make a motion?

TRUEWIT.

Briefly. For I must strike while 'tis hot.

CLERIMONT.

Shall I go fetch the ladies to the catastrophe?

TRUEWIT.

Umh? Ay, by my troth.

DAUPHINE.

By no mortal means. Let them continue in the state of ignorance, and err still; think 'em wits and fine fellows as they have done. 'Twere sin to reform them.

TRUEWIT.

Well, I will have 'em fetched, now I think on't, for a private purpose of mine; do, Clerimont, fetch 'em, and discourse to 'em all that's past, and bring 'em into the gallery here.

DAUPHINE.

This is thy extreme vanity now; thou think'st thou wert undone if every jest thou mak'st were not published.

TRUEWIT.

Thou shalt see how unjust thou art presently. Clerimont, say it was Dauphine's plot. {Exit Clerimont.} Trust me not if the whole drift be not for thy good. There's a carpet i' the next room; put it on, with this scarf over thy face and a cushion o' thy head, and be ready when I call Amorous. Away. {Exit Dauphine.} – John Daw! {Brings Daw out of his study.}

DAW.

What good news, sir?

TRUEWIT.

Faith, I have followed and argued with him hard for you. I told him you were a knight and a scholar, and that you knew fortitude did consist magis patiendo quam faciendo, magis ferendo quam feriendo.

DAW.

It doth so indeed, sir.

TRUEWIT.

And that you would suffer, I told him: so at first he demanded, by my troth, in my conceit too much.

DAW.

What was it, sir?

TRUEWIT.

Your upper lip, and six o' your fore-teeth.

DAW.

'Twas unreasonable.

TRUEWIT.

Nay, I told him plainly, you could not spare 'em all. So after long argument – pro et con, as you know – I brought him down to your two butter-teeth, and them he would have.

DAW.

Oh, did you so? Why, he shall have 'em.

{Enter above Haughty, Centaure, Mavis, Mistress Otter, Epicoene, Trusty, and Clerimont.}

TRUEWIT.

But he shall not, sir, by your leave. The conclusion is this, sir: because you shall be very good friends hereafter, and this never to be remembered or upbraided, besides that he may not boast he had done any such thing to you in his own person, he is to come here in disguise, give you five kicks in private, sir, take your sword from you, and lock you up in that study, during pleasure. Which will be but a little while, we'll get it released presently.

DAW.

Five kicks? He shall have six, sir, to be friends.

TRUEWIT.

Believe me, you shall not overshoot yourself to send him that word by me.

DAW.

Deliver it, sir. He shall have it with all my heart, to be friends.

TRUEWIT.

Friends? Nay, and he should not be so, and heartily too, upon these terms, he shall have me to enemy while I live. Come, sir, bear it bravely.

DAW.

Oh God, sir, 'tis nothing.

TRUEWIT.

True. What's six kicks to a man that reads Seneca?

DAW.

I have had a hundred, sir.

TRUEWIT.

Sir Amorous! No speaking one to another, or rehearsing old matter.

Dauphine comes forth and kicks him.

DAW.

One, two, three, four, five. I protest, Sir Amorous, you shall have six.

TRUEWIT.

Nay, I told you, you should not talk. Come, give him six, and he will needs. {*Dauphine kicks him again.*} Your sword. {*Daw gives Truewit his sword.*} Now return to your safe custody: you shall presently meet afore the ladies, and be the dearest friends one to another. {*Daw goes into his study.*} – Give me the scarf; now thou shalt beat the other barefaced. Stand by. {*Exit Dauphine.*} – Sir Amorous! {*Brings out La Foole.*}

LA FOOLE.

What's here? A sword¹

TRUEWIT.

I cannot help it, without I should take the quarrel upon myself; here he has sent you his sword –

LA FOOLE.

I'll receive none on't.

TRUEWIT.

And he wills you to fasten it against a wall, and break your head in some few several places against the hilts.

LA FOOLE.

I will not: tell him roundly. I cannot endure to shed my own blood.

TRUEWIT.

Will you not?

LA FOOLE.

No. I'll beat it against a fair flat wall, if that will satisfy him; if not, he shall beat it himself for Amorous.

TRUEWIT.

Why, this is strange starting off when a man undertakes for you! I offered him another condition: will you stand to that?

LA FOOLE.

Ay, what is't?

TRUEWIT.

That you will be beaten in private.

LA FOOLE.

Yes. I am content, at the blunt.

TRUEWIT.

Then you must submit yourself to be hoodwinked in this scarf, and be led to him, where he will take your sword from you, and make you bear a blow over the mouth, gules, and tweaks by the nose *sans nombre.*

LA FOOLE.

I am content. But why must I be blinded?

TRUEWIT.

That's for your good, sir: because if he should grow insolent upon this and publish it hereafter to your disgrace – which I hope he will not do – you might swear safely and protest he never beat you, to your knowledge.

LA FOOLE.

Oh, I conceive.

TRUEWIT.

I do not doubt but you'll be perfect good friends upon't, and not dare to utter an ill thought one of another in future.

LA FOOLE.

Not I, as God help me, of him.

TRUEWIT.

Nor he of you, sir. If he should – Come, sir. {*Blindfolds him.*}

– All hid, Sir John.

Dauphine enters to tweak him.

LA FOOLE.

Oh, Sir John, Sir John! Oh, o-o-o-o-o-Oh – {*Dauphine takes his sword.*}

TRUEWIT.

Good Sir John, leave tweaking, you'll blow his nose off. {*Exit Dauphine with the two swords.*} 'Tis Sir John's pleasure you should retire into the study. {*Unbinds La Foole's eyes and shuts him in.*} Why, now you are friends. All bitterness between you, I hope, is buried; you shall come forth by and by Damon and Pythias upon't, and embrace with all the rankness of friendship that can be.

{*Enter Dauphine.*}

I trust we shall have 'em tamer i' their language hereafter. Dauphine, I worship thee. – God's will, the ladies have surprised us!

ACT FOUR

Scene Six

{*Enter from above.*} Haughty, Centaure, Mavis, Mistress Otter, *Epicoene, Trusty, {and Clerimont,} having discovered part of the past scene above.*

HAUGHTY.

Centaure, how our judgements were imposed on by these adulterate knights!

CENTAURE.

Nay, madam, Mavis was more deceived than we; 'twas her commendation uttered 'em in the college.

MAVIS.

I commended but their wits, madam, and their braveries. I never looked toward their valours.

HAUGHTY.

Sir Dauphine is valiant, and a wit too, it seems.

MAVIS.

And a Bravery too.

HAUGHTY.

Was this his project?

MISTRESS OTTER.

So Master Clerimont intimates, madam.

HAUGHTY.

Good Morose, when you come to the college, will you bring him with you? He seems a very perfect gentleman.

EPICOENE.

He is so, madam, believe it.

CENTAURE.

But when will you come, Morose?

EPICOENE.

Three of four days hence, madam, when I have got me a coach and horses.

HAUGHTY.

No, tomorrow, good Morose; Centaure shall send you her coach.

MAVIS.

Yes, faith, do, and bring Sir Dauphine with you.

HAUGHTY.

She has promised that, Mavis.

MAVIS.

He is a very worthy gentlemen in his exteriors, madam.

HAUGHTY.

Ay, he shows he is judicial in his clothes.

CENTAURE.

And yet not so superlatively neat as some, madam, that have their faces set in a brake!

HAUGHTY.

Ay, and have every hair in form!

MAVIS.

That wear purer linen than ourselves, and profess more neatness than the French hermaphrodite!

EPICOENE.

Ay, ladies, they, what they tell one of us, have told a thousand, and are the only thieves of our fame, that think to take us with that perfume or with that lace, and laugh at us unconsciously when they have done.

HAUGHTY.

But Sir Dauphine's carelessness becomes him.

CENTAURE.

I could love a man for such a nose!

MAVIS.

Or such a leg!

CENTAURE.

He has an exceeding good eye, madam!

MAVIS.

And a very good lock!

CENTAURE.

Good Morose, bring him to my chamber first.

MISTRESS OTTER.

Please your honours to meet at my house, madam?

TRUEWIT.

{*Aside to Dauphine*}. See how they eye thee, man! They are taken, I warrant thee.

HAUGHTY.

{*Approaching Truewit and Dauphine*}. You have unbraced our brace of knights here, Master Truewit.

TRUEWIT.

Not I, madam, it was Sir Dauphine's engine; who, if he have disfurnished your ladyship of any guard or service by it, is able to make the place good again in himself.

HAUGHTY.

There's no suspicion of that, sir.

CENTAURE.

God so, Mavis, Haughty is kissing.

MAVIS.

Let us go too and take part.

HAUGHTY.

But I am glad of the fortune – beside the discovery of two such empty caskets – to gain the knowledge of so rich a mine of virtue as Sir Dauphine.

CENTAURE.

We would be all glad to style him of our friendship, and see him at the college.

MAVIS.

He cannot mix with a sweeter society, I'll prophesy, and I hope he himself will think so.

DAUPHINE.

I should be rude to imagine otherwise, lady.

TRUEWIT.

{*Aside to Dauphine*}. Did not I tell thee, Dauphine? Why, all their actions are governed by crude opinion, without reason or cause; they know not why they do anything; but as they are informed, believe, judge, praise, condemn, love, hate, and in emulation one of another, do all these things alike. Only, they have a natural inclination sways 'em generally to the worst, when they are left to themselves. But pursue it, now thou hast 'em.

HAUGHTY.

Shall we go in again, Morose?

EPICOENE.

Yes, madam.

CENTAURE.

We'll entreat Sir Dauphine's company.

TRUEWIT.

Stay, good madam, the interview of the two friends, Pylades and Orestes: I'll fetch 'em out to you straight.

HAUGHTY.

Will you, Master Truewit?

DAUPHINE.

Ay, but, noble ladies, do not confess in your countenance or outward bearing to 'em any discovery of their follies, that we may see how they will bear up again, with what assurance and erection.

HAUGHTY.

We will not, Sir Dauphine.

CLERIMONT {*and*} MAVIS.

Upon our honours, Sir Dauphine

TRUEWIT.

Sir Amorous, Sir Amorous! The ladies are here.

LA FOOLE.

{*Within*}. Are they?

TRUEWIT.

Yes, but slip out by and by as their backs are turned and meet Sir John here, as by chance, when I call you. – Jack Daw!

DAW.

(*Within*). What say you, sir?

TRUEWIT.

Whip out behind me suddenly, and no anger i' your looks to your adversary. – Now, now!

{*La Foole and Daw come out of their studies and salute each other.*}

LA FOOLE.

Noble Sir John Daw! Where ha' you been?

DAW.

To seek you, Sir Amorous.

LA FOOLE.

Me! I honour you.

DAW.

I prevent you, sir.

CLERIMONT.

They have forgot their rapiers!

TRUEWIT.

Oh, they meet in peace, man.

DAUPHINE.

Where's your sword, Sir John?

CLERIMONT.

And yours, Sir Amorous?

DAW.

Mine? My boy had it forth to mend the handle, e'en now.

LA FOOLE.

And my gold handle was broke too, and my boy had it forth.

DAUPHINE.

Indeed, sir? How their excuses meet!

CLERIMONT.

What a consent there is i' the handles!

TRUEWIT.

Nay, there is so i' the points too, I warrant you.

MISTRESS OTTER.

Oh me! Madam, he comes again, the madman! Away!

{*Exeunt hastily Haughty, Centaure, Epicoene, Mavis, Mistress Otter, Trusty, Daw, and La Foole.*}

ACT FOUR

Scene Seven

{*Enter*} Morose {*with a sword in each hand;*} *he had found the two swords drawn within.*

MOROSE.

What make these naked weapons here, gentlemen?

TRUEWIT.

Oh sir! Here hath like to been murder since you went! A couple of knights fallen out about the bride's favours. We were fain to take away their weapons, your house had been begged by this time else –

MOROSE.

For what?

CLERIMONT.

For manslaughter, sir, as being accessary.

MOROSE.

And for her favours?

TRUEWIT.

Ay, sir, heretofore, not present. Clerimont, carry 'em their swords now. They have done all the hurt they will do.

{*Exit Clerimont with the swords.*}

DAUPHINE.

Ha' you spoke with a lawyer, sir?

MOROSE.

Oh no! There is such a noise i' the court that they have frighted me home with more violence than I went! Such speaking and counter-speaking, with their several voices of citations, appellations, allegations, certificates, attachments, intergatories, references, convictions, and afflictions indeed among the doctors and proctors, that the noise here is silence to't! A kind of calm midnight!

TRUEWIT.

Why, sir, if you would be resolved indeed, I can bring you hither a very sufficient lawyer and a learned divine, that shall enquire into every least scruple for you.

MOROSE.

Can you, Master Truewit?

TRUEWIT.

Yes, and are very sober grave persons, that will dispatch it in a chamber, with a whisper or two.

MOROSE.

Good sir, shall I hope this benefit from you, and trust myself into your hands?

TRUEWIT.

Alas, sir! Your nephew and I have been ashamed, and oft-times mad, since you went, to think how you are abused.

Go in, good sir, and lock yourself up till we call you; we'll tell you more anon, sir.

MOROSE.

Do your pleasure with me, gentlemen; I believe in you, and that deserves no delusion –

TRUEWIT.

You shall find none, sir {*Exit Morose.*} – but heaped, heaped plenty of vexation.

DAUPHINE.

What wilt thou do now, Wit?

TRUEWIT.

Recover me hither Otter and the barber if you can, by any means, presently.

DAUPHINE.

Why? To what purpose?

TRUEWIT.

Oh, I'll make the deepest divine and gravest lawyer out o' them two for him –

DAUPHINE.

Thou canst not, man; these are waking dreams.

TRUEWIT.

Do not fear me. Clap but a civil gown with a welt o' the one, and a canonical cloak with sleeves o' the other, and give 'em a few terms i' their mouths; if there come not forth as able a doctor and complete a parson for this turn as may be wished, trust not my election. And I hope, without wronging the dignity of either profession, since they are but persons put on, and for mirth's sake, to torment him. The barber smatters Latin, I remember.

DAUPHINE.

Yes, and Otter too.

TRUEWIT.

Well then, if I make 'em not wrangle out this case to his no comfort, let me be thought a Jack Daw, or La Foole, or anything worse. Go you to your ladies, but first send for them.

DAUPHINE.

I will.

{*Exeunt.*}

ACT FIVE

Scene One

{*Enter*} *La Foole, Clerimont, Daw.*

LA FOOLE.

Where had you our swords, Master Clerimont?

CLERIMONT.

Why, Dauphine took 'em from the madman.

LA FOOLE.

And he took 'em from our boys, I warrant you.

CLERIMONT.

Very like, sir.

LA FOOLE.

Thank you, good Master Clerimont. Sir John Daw and I are both beholden to you.

CLERIMONT.

Would I knew how to make you so, gentlemen.

DAW.

Sir Amorous and I are your servants, sir.

{*Enter Mavis.*}

MAVIS.

Gentlemen, have any of you a pen and ink? I would fain write out a riddle in Italian for Sir Dauphine to translate.

CLERIMONT.

Not I, in troth, lady, I am no scrivener.

DAW.

I can furnish you, I think, lady.

{*Exeunt Daw and Mavis.*}

CLERIMONT.

He has it in the haft of a knife, I believe!

LA FOOLE.

No, he has his box of instruments.

CLERIMONT.

Like a surgeon!

LA FOOLE.

For the mathematics: his squire, his compasses, his brass pens, and black lead, to draw maps of every place and person where he comes.

CLERIMONT.
How, maps of persons!

LA FOOLE.
Yes, sir, of Nomentack, when he was here, and of the Prince of Moldavia, and of his mistress, Mistress Epicoene.

CLERIMONT.
Away! He has not found out her latitude, I hope.

LA FOOLE.
You are a pleasant gentleman, sir.

{Enter Daw.}

CLERIMONT.
Faith, now we are in private, let's wanton it a little and talk waggishly. Sir John, I am telling Sir Amorous here that you two govern the ladies; where'er you come, you carry the feminine gender afore you.

DAUPHINE.
They shall rather carry us afore them, if they will, sir.

CLERIMONT.
Nay, I believe that they do, withal; but that you are the prime men in their affections, and direct all their actions –

DAW.
Not I; Sir Amorous is.

LA FOOLE.
I protest Sir John is.

DAW.
As I hope to rise i' the state, Sir Amorous, you ha' the person.

LA FOOLE.
Sir John, you ha' the person, and the discourse too.

DAW.
Not I, sir. I have no discourse – and then you have activity beside.

LA FOOLE.
I protest, Sir John, you come as high from Tripoli as I do every whit, and lift as many joined stools and leap over 'em, if you would use it –

CLERIMONT.
Well, agree on't together, knights, for between you you divide the kingdom or commonwealth of ladies' affections: I see it and can perceive a little how they observe you, and fear you, indeed. You could tell strange stories, my masters, if you

would, I know.

DAW.
Faith, we have seen somewhat, sir.

LA FOOLE.
That we have: vellet petticoats and wrought smocks or so.

DAW.
Ay, and –

CLERIMONT.
Nay, out with it, Sir John; do not envy your friend the pleasure of hearing, when you have had the delight of tasting.

DAW.
Why – a – do you speak, Sir Amorous.

LA FOOLE.
No, do you, Sir John Daw.

DAW.
I' faith, you shall.

LA FOOLE.
I' faith, you shall.

DAW.
Why, we have been –

LA FOOLE.
In the great bed at Ware together in our time. On, Sir John.

DAW.
Nay, do you, Sir Amorous.

CLERIMONT.
And these ladies with you, knights?

LA FOOLE.
No, excuse us, sir.

DAW.
We must not wound reputation.

LA FOOLE.
No matter; they were these, or others. Our bath cost us fifteen pound, when we came home.

CLERIMONT.
Do you hear, Sir John, you shall tell me but one thing truly, as you love me.

DAW.
If I can, I will, sir.

CLERIMONT.

You lay in the same house with the bride here?

DAW.

Yes, and conversed with her hourly, sir.

CLERIMONT.

And what humour is she of? Is she coming and open, free?

DAW.

Oh, exceeding open, sir. I was her servant, and Sir Amorous was to be.

CLERIMONT.

Come, you have both had favours from her? I know and have heard so much.

DAW.

Oh no, sir.

LA FOOLE.

You shall excuse us, sir: we must not wound reputation.

CLERIMONT.

Tut, she is married now, and you cannot hurt her with any report, and therefore speak plainly: how many times, i' faith? Which of you led first? Ha?

LA FOOLE.

Sir John had her maidenhead, indeed.

DAW.

Oh, it pleases him to say so, sir, but Sir Amorous knows what's what as well.

CLERIMONT.

Dost thou i' faith, Amorous?

LA FOOLE.

In a manner, sir.

CLERIMONT.

Why, I commend you, lads. Little knows Don Bridegroom of this. Nor shall he, for me.

DAW.

Hang him, mad ox.

CLERIMONT.

Speak softly: here comes his nephew, with the Lady Haughty. He'll get the ladies from you, sirs, if you look not to him in time.

LA FOOLE.

Why if he do, we'll fetch 'em home again, I warrant you.

{*Exeunt.*}

ACT FIVE

Scene Two

{*Enter*} Haughty, Dauphine.

HAUGHTY.

I assure you, Sir Dauphine, it is the price and estimation of your virtue only that hath embarked me to this adventure, and I could not but make out to tell you so; nor can I repent me of the act, since it is always an argument of some virtue in ourselves that we love and affect it so in others.

DAUPHINE.

Your ladyship sets too high a price on my weakness.

HAUGHTY.

Sir, I can distinguish gems from pebbles –

DAUPHINE.

Are you so skilful in stones?

HAUGHTY.

And howsoever I may suffer in such a judgement as yours, by admitting equality of rank or society with Centaure or Mavis –

DAUPHINE.

You do not, madam; I perceive they are your mere foils.

HAUGHTY.

Then are you a friend to truth, sir. It makes me love you the more. It is not the outward but the inward man that I affect. They are not apprehensive of an eminent perfection, but love flat and dully.

CENTAURE

{*Within*}. Where are you, my Lady Haughty?

HAUGHTY.

I come presently, Centaure. – My chamber, sir, my page shall show you; and Trusty, my woman, shall be ever awake for you; you need not fear to communicate anything with her, for she is a Fidelia. I pray you wear this jewel for my sake, Sir Dauphine.

{*Enter Centaure.*}

Where's Mavis, Centaure?

CENTAURE.
Within, madam, a-writing. I'll follow you presently. I'll but speak a word with Sir Dauphine.

{Exit Haughty.}

DAUPHINE.
With me, madam?

CENTAURE.
Good Sir Dauphine, do not trust Haughty, nor make any credit to her, whatever you do besides. Sir Dauphine, I give you this caution, she is a perfect courtier and loves nobody but for her uses, and for her uses she loves all. Besides, her physicians give her out to be none o' the clearest – whether she pay 'em or no, heav'n knows; and she's above fifty too, and pargets! See her in a forenoon. Here comes Mavis, a worse face than she! You would not like this by candlelight. If you'll come to my chamber one o' these mornings early, or late in an evening, I'll tell you more.

{Enter Mavis.}

Where's Haughty, Mavis?

MAVIS.
Within, Centaure.

CENTAURE.
What ha' you there?

MAVIS.
An Italian riddle for Sir Dauphine. – You shall not see it i' faith, Centaure. – Good Sir Dauphine, solve it for me. I'll call for it anon.

{Exeunt Mavis and Centaure.}

{Enter Clerimont.}

CLERIMONT.
How now, Dauphine? How dost thou quit thyself of these females?

DAUPHINE.
'Slight, they haunt me like fairies, and give me jewels here; I cannot be rid of 'em.

CLERIMONT.
Oh, you must not tell though.

DAUPHINE.
Mass, I forgot that; I was never so assaulted. One loves for virtue, and bribes me with this. Another loves me with caution, and so would possess me. A third brings me a riddle here, and all are jealous and rail each at other.

CLERIMONT.
A riddle? Pray' le' me see't? (He reads the paper.) 'Sir Dauphine, I chose this way of intimation for privacy. The ladies here, I know, have both hope and purpose to make a collegiate and servant of you. If I might be so honoured as to appear at any end of so noble a work, I would enter into a fame of taking physic tomorrow and continue it four or five days or longer, for your visitation. Mavis.' – By my faith, a subtle one! Call you this a riddle? What's their plain dealing, trow?

DAUPHINE.
We lack Truewit to tell us that.

CLERIMONT.
We lack him for somewhat else too: his knights reformados are wound up as high and insolent as ever they were.

DAUPHINE.
You jest.

CLERIMONT.
No drunkards, either with wine or vanity, ever confessed such stories of themselves. I would not give a fly's leg in balance against all the women's reputations here, if they could be but thought to speak truth; and for the bride, they have made their affidavit against her directly –

DAUPHINE.
What, that they have lien with her?

CLERIMONT.
Yes, and tell times and circumstances, with the cause why and the place where. I had almost brought 'em to affirm that they had done it today.

DAUPHINE.
Not both of 'em.

CLERIMONT.
Yes, faith; with a sooth or two more I had effected it. They would ha' set it down under their hands.

DAUPHINE.
Why, they will be our sport, I see, still! whether we will or no.

ACT FIVE

Scene Three

{*Enter*} *Truewit.*

TRUEWIT.

Oh, are you here? Come, Dauphine. Go call your uncle presently. I have fitted my divine and my canonist, dyed their beards and all; the knaves do not know themselves, they are so exalted and altered. Preferment changes any man. Thou shalt keep one door and I another, and then Clerimont in the midst, that he may have no means of escape from their cavilling when they grow hot once. And then the women – as I have given the bride her instructions – to break in upon him i' the *l'envoy*. Oh, 'twill be full and twanging! Away, fetch him.

{*Exit Dauphine.*}

{*Enter Cutbeard disguised as a canon lawyer, Otter as a divine.*}

Come, master doctor and master parson, look to your parts now and discharge 'em bravely; you are well set forth, perform it as well. If you chance to be out, do not confess it with standing still or humming or gaping one at another, but go on and talk aloud and eagerly, use vehement action, and only remember your terms, and you are safe. Let the matter go where it will: you have many will do so. But at first be very solemn and grave like your garments, though you loose yourselves after and skip out like a brace of jugglers on a table. Here he comes! Set your faces, and look superciliously while I present you.

{*Enter Dauphine and Morose.*}

MOROSE.

Are these the two learned men?

TRUEWIT.

Yes, sir: please you salute 'em?

MOROSE.

Salute 'em? I had rather do anything than wear out time so unfruitfully, sir. I wonder how these common forms, as 'God save you' and 'You are welcome', are come to be a habit in our lives! Or 'I am glad to see you'! when I cannot see what the profit can be of these words, so long as it is no whit better with him whose affairs are sad and grievous that he hears this salutation.

TRUEWIT.

'Tis true, sir; we'll go to the matter then. Gentlemen, master doctor and master parson, I have acquainted you sufficiently with the business for which you are come hither. And you are not now to inform yourselves in the state of the question, I know. This is the gentleman who expects your resolution, and therefore, when you please, begin.

OTTER.

Please you, master doctor.

CUTBEARD.

Please you, good master parson.

OTTER.

I would hear the canon law speak first.

CUTBEARD.

It must give place to positive divinity, sir.

MOROSE.

Nay, good gentlemen, do not throw me into circumstances. Let your comforts arrive quickly at me, those that are. Be swift in affording me my peace, if so I shall hope any. I love not your disputations or your court tumults. And that it be not strange to you, I will tell you. My father, in my education, was wont to advise me that I should always collect and contain my mind, not suff'ring it to flow loosely; that I should look to what things were necessary to the carriage of my life, and what not, embracing the one and eschewing the other. In short, that I should endear myself to rest and avoid turmoil, which now is grown to be another nature to me. So that I come not to your public pleadings or your places of noise; not that I neglect those things that make for the dignity of the commonwealth, but for the mere avoiding of clamours and impertinencies of orators, that know not how to be silent. And for the cause of noise am I now a suitor to you. You do not know in what a misery I have been exercised this day, what a torrent of evil! My very house turns round with the tumult! I dwell in a windmill! The perpetual motion is here, and not at Eltham.

TRUEWIT.

Well, good master doctor, will you break the ice? Master parson will wade after.

CUTBEARD.

Sir, though unworthy, and the weaker, I will presume.

OTTER.

'Tis no presumption, *domine* doctor.

MOROSE.

Yet again!

CUTBEARD.

Your question is, for how many causes a man may have *divortium legitimum*, a lawful divorce. First, you must understand the nature of the word divorce, *a divertendo* –

MOROSE.

No excursions upon words, good doctor; to the question briefly.

CUTBEARD.

I answer then, the canon law affords divorce but in few cases, and the principal is in the common case, the adulterous case. But there are *duodecim impedimenta*, twelve impediments – as we call 'em – all which do not *dirimere contractum*, but *irritum reddere matrimonium*, as we say in the canon law, not take away the bond, but cause a nullity therein.

MOROSE.

I understood you before; good sir, avoid your impertinency of translation.

OTTER.

He cannot open this too much, sir, by your favour.

MOROSE.

Yet more!

TRUEWIT.

Oh, you must give the learned men leave, sir. To your impediments, master doctor.

CUTBEARD.

The first is *impedimentum erroris*.

OTTER.

Of which there are several species.

CUTBEARD.

Ay, as *error personae*.

OTTER.

If you contract yourself to one person, thinking her another.

CUTBEARD.

Then, *error fortunae*.

OTTER.

If she be a beggar, and you thought her rich.

CUTBEARD.

Then, *error qualitatis*.

OTTER.

If she prove stubborn or headstrong, that you thought obedient.

MOROSE.

How? Is that, sir, a lawful impediment? One at once, I pray, you, gentlemen.

OTTER.

Ay, *ante copulam*, but not *post copulam*, sir.

CUTBEARD.

Master parson says right. *Nec post nuptiarum benedictionem*. It doth indeed but *irrita reddere sponsalia*, annul the contract; after marriage it is of no obstancy.

TRUEWIT.

Alas, sir, what a hope we are fall'n from, by this time!

CUTBEARD.

The next is *conditio*: if you thought her free-born, and she prove a bondwoman, there is impediment of estate and condition.

OTTER.

Ay, but master doctor, those servitudes are *sublatae* now, among us Christians.

CUTBEARD.

By your favour, master parson –

OTTER.

You shall give me leave, master doctor.

MOROSE.

Nay, gentlemen, quarrel not in that question; it concerns not my case: pass to the third.

CUTBEARD.

Well then, the third is *votum*. If either party have made a vow of chastity. But that practice, as master parson said of the other, is taken away among us, thanks be to discipline. The fourth is *cognatio*: if the persons be of kin within the degrees.

OTTER.

Ay. Do you know what the degrees are, sir?

MOROSE.

No, nor I care not, sir; they offer me no comfort in the question, I am sure.

CUTBEARD.

But there is a branch of this impediment may, which is *cognatio spiritualis*. If you were her godfather, sir, then the marriage is incestuous.

OTTER.

That comment is absurd and superstitious, master doctor. I cannot endure it. Are we not all brothers and sisters, and as much akin in that as godfathers and god-daughters?

MOROSE.

Oh me! To end the controversy, I never was a godfather, I never was a godfather in my life, sir. Pass to the next.

CUTBEARD.

The fifth is *crimen adulterii*: the known case. The sixth, *cultus disparitas*, difference of religion: have you ever examined her what religion she is of?

MOROSE.

No, I would rather she were of none, than be put to the trouble of it!

OTTER.

You may have it done for you, sir.

MOROSE.

By no means, good sir; on to the rest. Shall you ever come to an end, think you?

TRUEWIT.

Yes, he has done half, sir. – On to the rest. – Be patient and expect, sir.

CUTBEARD.

The seventh is *vis*: if it were upon compulsion or force.

MOROSE.

Oh no, it was too voluntary, mine; too voluntary.

CUTBEARD.

The eighth is *ordo*: if ever she have taken holy orders.

OTTER.

That's superstitious too.

MOROSE.

No matter, master parson: would she would go into a nunnery yet.

CUTBEARD.

The ninth is *ligamen*: if you were bound, sir, to any other before.

MOROSE.

I thrust myself too soon into these fetters.

CUTBEARD.

The tenth is *publica honestas*, which is *inchoata quaedam affinitas*.

OTTER.

Ay, or *affinitas orta ex sponsalibus*, and is but *leve impedimentum*.

MOROSE.

I feel no air of comfort blowing to me in all this.

CUTBEARD.

The eleventh is *affinitas ex fornicatione*.

OTTER.

Which is no less *vera affinitas* than the other, master doctor.

CUTBEARD.

True, *quae oritur ex legitimo matrimonio*.

OTTER.

You say right, venerable doctor. And *nascitur ex eo, quod per conjugium duae personae efficiuntur una caro* –

MOROSE.

Heyday, now they begin!

CUTBEARD.

I conceive you, master parson. *Ita per fornicationem aeque est verus pater, qui sic generat* –

OTTER.

Et vere filius qui sic generatur –

MOROSE.What's all this to me?

CLERIMONT

{*Aside*}. Now it grows warm.

CUTBEARD.

The twelfth and last is *si forte coire nequibis*.

OTTER.

Ay, that is *impedimentum gravissimum*. It doth utterly annul and annihilate, that. If you have *manifestam frigiditatem*, you are well, sir.

TRUEWIT.

Why, there is comfort come at length, sir. Confess yourself but a man unable, and she will sue to be divorced first.

OTTER.

Ay, or if there be *morbus perpetuus et insanabilis*, as paralysis, elephantiasis, or so –

DAUPHINE.

Oh, but *frigiditas* is the fairer way, gentlemen.

OTTER.

You say troth, sir, and as it is in the canon, master doctor.

CUTBEARD.

I conceive you, sir.

CLERIMONT.

{*Aside*}. Before he speaks.

OTTER.

That 'a boy or child under years is not fit for marriage because he cannot *reddere debitum*'. So your *omnipotentes* –

TRUEWIT.

{*Aside to Otter*}. Your *impotentes*, you whoreson lobster.

OTTER.

Your *impotentes*, I should say, are *minime apti ad contrahenda matrimomium*.

TRUEWIT.

{*Aside to Otter*}. *Matrimonium*? We shall have most unmatrimonial Latin with you: *matrimonia*, and be hanged.

DAUPHINE.

{*Aside to Truewit*}.You put 'em out, man.

CUTBEARD.

But then there will arise a doubt, master parson, in our case, *post matrimonium*: that *frigiditate praeditus* – do you conceive me, sir?

OTTER.

Very well, sir.

CUTBEARD.

Who cannot *uti uxore pro uxore*, may *habere eam pro sorore*.

OTTER.

Absurd, absurd, absurd, and merely apostatical.

CUTBEARD.

You shall pardon me, master parson, I can prove it.

OTTER.

You can prove a will, master doctor, you can prove nothing else. Does not the verse of your own canon say, *Haec socianda vetant conubia, facta retractant* –

CUTBEARD.

I grant you, but how do they *retractare*, master parson?

MOROSE.

Oh, this was it I feared.

OTTER.

In aeternum, sir.

CUTBEARD.

That's false in divinity, by your favour.

OTTER.

'Tis false in humanity to say so. Is he not *prorsus inutilis ad thorum*? Can he *praestare fidem datam*? I would fain know.

CUTBEARD.

Yes: how if we do *convalere*?

OTTER.

He cannot *convalere*, it is impossible.

TRUEWIT.

{*To Morose*}. Nay, good sir, attend the learned men; they'll think you neglect 'em else.

CUTBEARD.

Or if he do *simulare* himself *frigidum, odio uxoris*, or so?

OTTER.

I say he is *adulter manifestus* then.

DAUPHINE.

They dispute it very learnedly, i' faith.

OTTER.

And *prostitutor uxoris*, and this is positive.

MOROSE.

Good sir, let me escape.

TRUEWIT.

You will not do me that wrong, sir?

OTTER.

And therefore, if he be *manifeste frigidus*, sir –

CUTBEARD.

Ay, if he be *manifeste frigidus*, I grant you –

OTTER.

Why, that was my conclusion.

CUTBEARD.

And mine too.

TRUEWIT.

Nay, hear the conclusion, sir.

OTTER.

Then *frigiditatis causa* –

CUTBEARD.

Yes, *causa frigiditatis* –

MOROSE.

Oh, mine ears!

OTTER.
She may have *libellum divortii* against you.

CUTBEARD.
Ay, *divortii libellum* she will sure have.

MOROSE.
Good echoes, forbear.

OTTER.
If you confess it.

CUTBEARD.
Which I would do, sir –

MOROSE.
I will do anything –

OTTER.
And clear myself *in foro conscientiae* –

CUTBEARD.
Because you want indeed –

MOROSE.
Yet more?

OTTER.
Exercendi potestate.

ACT FIVE

Scene Four

{Enter} *Epicoene, Haughty, Centaure, Mavis, Mistress Otter, Daw, La Foole.*

EPICOENE.
I will not endure it any longer! Ladies, I beseech you help me. This is such a wrong as never was offered to poor bride before. Upon her marriage-day, to have her husband conspire against her, and a couple of mercenary companions to be brought in for form's sake, to persuade a separation! If you had blood or virtue in you, gentlemen, you would not suffer such earwigs about a husband, or scorpions to creep between man and wife –

MOROSE.
Oh the variety and changes of my torment!

HAUGHTY.
Let 'em be cudgelled out of doors by our grooms.

CENTAURE.
I'll lend you my footman.

MAVIS.
We'll have our men blanket 'em i' the hall.

MISTRESS OTTER.
As there was one at our house, madam, for peeping in at the door.

DAW.
Content, i' faith.

TRUEWIT.
Stay, ladies and gentlemen, you'll hear before you proceed?

MAVIS.
I'd ha' the bridegroom blanketed too.

CENTAURE.
Begin with him first.

HAUGHTY.
Yes, by my troth.

MOROSE.
Oh mankind generation!

DAUPHINE.
Ladies, for my sake forbear.

HAUGHTY.
Yes, for Sir Dauphine's sake.

CENTAURE.
He shall command us.

LA FOOLE.
He is as fine a gentleman of his inches, madam, as any is about the town, and wears as good colours when he list.

TRUEWIT.
{aside to Morose}.
Be brief, sir, and confess your infirmity, she'll be afire to be quit of you; if she but hear that named once, you shall not entreat her to stay. She'll fly you like one that had the marks upon him.

MOROSE.
Ladies, I must crave all your pardons –

TRUEWIT.
Silence, ladies.

MOROSE.

For a wrong I have done to your whole sex in marrying this fair and virtuous gentlewoman –

CLERIMONT.

Hear him, good ladies.

MOROSE.

Being guilty of an infirmity which, before I conferred with these learned men, I thought I might have concealed –

TRUEWIT.

But now being better informed in his conscience by them, he is to declare it and give satisfaction by asking your public forgiveness.

MOROSE.

I am no man, ladies.

ALL.

How!

MOROSE.

Utterly unabled in nature, by reason of frigidity, to perform the duties or any the least office of a husband.

MAVIS.

Now out upon him, prodigious creature!

CENTAURE.

Bridegroom uncarnate.

HAUGHTY.

And would you offer it, to a young gentlewoman?

MISTRESS OTTER.

A lady of her longings?

EPICOENE.

Tut, a device, a device, this, it smells rankly, ladies. A mere comment of his own.

TRUEWIT.

Why, if you suspect that, ladies, you may have him searched.

DAW.

As the custom is, by a jury of physicians.

LA FOOLE.

Yes, faith, 'twill be brave.

MOROSE.

Oh me, must I undergo that!

MISTRESS OTTER.

No, let women search him, madam: we can do it ourselves.

MOROSE.

Out on me, worse!

EPICOENE.

No, ladies, you shall not need, I'll take him with all his faults.

MOROSE.

Worst of all!

CLERIMONT.

Why, then 'tis no divorce, doctor, if she consent not?

CUTBEARD.

No, if the man be *frigidus*, it is *de parte uxoris* that we grant *libellum divortii*, in the law.

OTTER.

Ay, it is the same in theology.

MOROSE.

Worse, worse than worst!

TRUEWIT.

Nay, sir, be not utterly disheartened, we have yet a small relic of hope left, as near as our comfort is blown out. {*Aside to Clerimont.*} Clerimont, produce your brace of knights. – What was that, master parson, you told me *in errore qualitatis*, e'en now? {*Aside to Dauphine.*} Dauphine, whisper the bride that she carry it as if she were guilty and ashamed.

OTTER.

Marry, sir, *in errore qualitatis* – which master doctor did forbear to urge – if she be found *corrupta*, that is, vitiated or broken up, that was *pro virgine desponsa*, espoused for a maid –

MOROSE.

What then, sir?

OTTER.

It doth *dirimere contractum* and *irritum reddere* too.

TRUEWIT.

If this be true, we are happy again, sir, once more. Here ar an honourable brace of knights that shall affirm so much.

DAW.

Pardon us, good Master Clerimont.

LA FOOLE.

You shall excuse us, Master Clerimont.

CLERIMONT.

Nay, you must make it good now, knights, there is remedy; I'll eat no words for you nor no men: you k

you spoke it to me?

DAW.

Is this gentleman-like, sir?

TRUEWIT.

{*Aside to Daw*}. Jack Daw, he's worse than Sir Amorous, fiercer a great deal. {*Aside to La Foole.*} Sir Amorous, beware, there be ten Daws in this Clerimont.

LA FOOLE.

I'll confess it, sir.

DAW.

Will you, Sir Amorous? Will you wound reputation?

LA FOOLE.

I am resolved.

TRUEWIT.

So should you be too, Jack Daw: what should keep you off? She is but a woman, and in disgrace. He'll be glad on't.

DAW.

Will he? I thought he would ha' been angry.

CLERIMONT.

You will dispatch, knights; it must be done, i' faith.

TRUEWIT.

Why, an' it must, it shall, sir, they say. They'll ne'er go back. {*Aside to Daw and La Foole.*} Do not tempt his patience.

DAW.

It is true indeed, sir.

LA FOOLE.

Yes, I assure you, sir.

MOROSE.

What is true, gentlemen? What do you assure me?

DAW.

That we have known your bride, sir –

LA FOOLE.

In good fashion. She was our mistress, or so –

CLERIMONT.

Nay, you must be plain, knights, as you were to me.

OTTER.

Ay, the question is, if you have *carnaliter* or no.

LA FOOLE.

Carnaliter? What else, sir?

OTTER.

It is enough: a plain nullity.

EPICOENE.

I am undone, I am undone!

MOROSE.

Oh, let me worship and adore you, gentlemen!

EPICOENE.

I am undone!

MOROSE.

Yes, to my hand, I thank these knights. Master parson, let me thank you otherwise. {*Gives Otter money.*}

CENTAURE.

And ha' they confessed?

MAVIS.

Now out upon 'em, informers!

TRUEWIT.

You see what creatures you may bestow your favours on, madams.

HAUGHTY.

I would except against 'em as beaten knights, wench, and not good witnesses in law.

MISTRESS OTTER.

Poor gentlewoman, how she takes it!

HAUGHTY.

Be comforted, Morose, I love you the better for't.

CENTAURE.

So do I, I protest.

CUTBEARD.

But, gentlemen, you have not known her since *matrimonium*?

DAW.

Not today, master doctor.

LA FOOLE.

No, sir, not today.

CUTBEARD.

Why, then I say, for any act before, the *matrimonium* is good and perfect, unless the worshipful bridegroom did precisely, before witness, demand if she were *virgo ante nuptias*.

EPICOENE.

No, that he did not, I assure you, master doctor.

CUTBEARD.

If he cannot prove that, it is *ratum conjugium*, notwithstanding the premises. And they do no way *impedire*. And this is my sentence, this I pronounce.

OTTER.

I am of master doctor's resolution too, sir, if you made not that demand *ante nuptias*.

MOROSE.

Oh my heart! Wilt thou break? Wilt thou break? This is worst of all worst worsts! that hell could have devised! Marry a whore! and so much noise!

DAUPHINE.

Come, I see now plain confederacy in this doctor and this parson, to abuse a gentleman. You study his affliction. I pray be gone, companions. And gentlemen, I begin to suspect you for having parts with 'em. Sir, will it please you hear me?

MOROSE.

Oh, do not talk to me, take not from me the pleasure of dying in silence, nephew.

DAUPHINE.

Sir, I must speak to you. I have been long your poor despised kinsman, and many a hard thought has strengthened you against me; but now it shall appear if either I love you or your peace, and prefer them to all the world beside. I will not be long or grievous to you, sir. If I free you of this unhappy match absolutely and instantly after all this trouble, and almost in your despair now –

MOROSE.

It cannot be.

DAUPHINE.

Sir, that you be never troubled with a murmur of it more, what shall I hope for or deserve of you?

MOROSE.

Oh, what thou wilt, nephew! Thou shalt deserve me and have me.

DAUPHINE.

Shall I have your favour perfect to me, and love hereafter?

MOROSE.

That and anything beside. Make thine own conditions. My whole estate is thine. Manage it, I will become thy ward.

DAUPHINE.

Nay, sir, I will not be so unreasonable

EPICOENE.

Will Sir Dauphine be mine enemy too?

DAUPHINE.

You know I have been long a suitor to you, uncle, that out of your estate, which is fifteen hundred a year, you would allow me but five hundred during life, and assure the rest upon me after, to which I have often by myself and friends tendered you a writing to sign, which you would never consent or incline to. If you please but to effect it now –

MOROSE.

Thou shalt have it, nephew. I will do it, and more.

DAUPHINE.

If I quit you not presently and forever of this cumber, you shall have power instantly, afore all these, to revoke your act, and I will become whose slave you will give me to forever.

MOROSE.

Where is the writing? I will seal to it, that, or to a blank, and write thine own conditions.

EPICOENE.

Oh me, most unfortunate wretched gentlewoman!

HAUGHTY.

Will Sir Dauphine do this?

EPICOENE.

Good sir, have some compassion on me. {*Weeps.*}

MOROSE.

Oh, my nephew knows you belike; away, crocodile!

CENTAURE.

He does it not, sure, without good ground.

DAUPHINE.

Here, sir. {*Gives him papers.*}

MOROSE.

Come, nephew, give me the pen. I will subscribe to anything, and seal to what thou wilt, for my deliverance. Thou art my restorer. Here, I deliver it thee as my deed. If there be a word in it lacking or writ with false orthography, I protest before – I will not take the advantage. {*Returns papers.*}

DAUPHINE.

Then here is your release, sir:

He takes off Epicoene's peruke.

you have married a boy: a gentleman's son that I have brought up this half year at my great charges, and for this composition which I have now made with you. – What say you, master doctor? This is *justum impedimentum*, I hope, *error personae*?

OTTER.

Yes, sir, *in primo gradu*.

CUTBEARD.

In primo gradu.

DAUPHINE.

I thank you, good Doctor Cutbeard and Parson Otter.

He pulls off their beards and disguise.

You are beholden to 'em, sir, that have taken this pains for you; and my friend, Master Truewit, who enabled 'em for the business. Now you may go in and rest, be as private as you will, sir. I'll not trouble you till you trouble me with your funeral, which I care not how soon it come.

{Exit Morose.}

Cutbeard, I'll make your lease good. Thank me not but with your leg, Cutbeard. And Tom Otter, your princess shall be reconciled to you. – How now, gentlemen! Do you look at me?

CLERIMONT.

A boy.

DAUPHINE.

Yes, Mistress Epicoene.

TRUEWIT.

Well, Dauphine, you have lurched your friends of the better half of the garland, by concealing this part of the plot! But much good do it thee, thou deserv'st it, lad. And Clerimont, for thy unexpected bringing in these two to confession, wear my part of it freely. Nay, Sir Daw and Sir La Foole, you see the gentlewoman that has done you the favours! We are all thankful to you, and so should the womankind here, specially for lying on her, though not with her! You meant so, I am sure? But that we have stuck it upon you today in your imagined persons, and so lately, this Amazon, the champion of the sex, should beat you now thriftily for the common slanders which ladies receive from such cuckoos as you are. You are they that, when no merit or fortune can make you hope to enjoy their bodies, will yet lie with their reputations and make their fame suffer. Away, you common moths of these and all ladies' honours. Go, travel to make legs and faces, and come home with some new matter to be laughed at: you deserve to live in an air as corrupted as that wherewith you feed rumour.

{Exeunt Daw and La Foole.}

Madams, you are mute upon this new metamorphosis! But here stands she that has vindicated your fames. Take heed of such *insectae* hereafter. And let it not trouble you that you have discovered any mysteries to this young gentleman. He is, a'most, of years, and will make a good visitant within this twelvemonth. In the meantime we'll all undertake for his secrecy, that can speak so well of his silence. *{Coming forward.}* Spectators, if you like this comedy, rise cheerfully, and now Morose is gone in, clap your hands. It may be that noise will cure him, at least please him.

{Exeunt.}